GLYPHS OF LOVE

Poetry and Paintings

Tendai Rinos Mwanaka

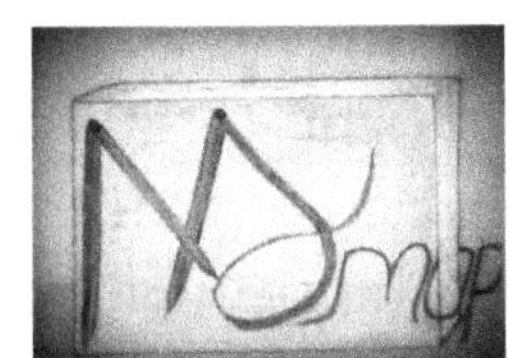

Mwanaka Media and Publishing Pvt Ltd,
Chitungwiza Zimbabwe
*
Creativity, Wisdom and Beauty

Publisher: MMAP
Mwanaka Media and Publishing Pvt Ltd *(Mmap)*
24 Svosve Road, Zengeza 1
Chitungwiza Zimbabwe
mwanaka@yahoo.com
www.africanbookscollective.com/publishers/mwanaka-media-and-publishing
https://facebook.com/MwanakaMediaAndPublishing/

Distributed in and outside N. America by African Books Collective
orders@africanbookscollective.com
www.africanbookscollective.com

ISBN: 9781779338617
EAN: 978-1-77933-861-7

DISCLAIMER

All views expressed in this publication are those of the author and do not necessarily reflect the views of *Mmap.*

Table of contents

He burns
UNNAMEABLE WOUND
Connection VI
Love means
MMAP MULTI DISCIPLINARY SERIES

Introduction

I always work around an idea, and create a group of works around the idea at a time. For this year I have tried to focus more on art and poetry, the combination of these in an interactive multidisciplinary style. This is the third book this year that combines visual art and poetry. I have since published, *of poets, gods, ghosts, irritants and storytellers: diagramatologically Unleashed* (which combined poetry, paintings, photography and some vignette essays) and *The Aporia of Unnamed Things* (which combines drawings and poetry responding or not responding to the drawings) and this one *Glyphs of Love* combines paintings and poetry. This is a collection of mostly love poems combined with symbolic renderings of mostly love-themed visual paintings. In these paintings you see, or seem to see the shapes, sometimes they disappear in the mazes. Most of the paintings are from my group of paintings I entitled *Connections*, thus you can see 4 painting entitled Connection. And this was what I wrote about these drawings about

"A relationship or association between people, a link between things. In the artworks we have connections or links between animals and humans, the earth and the atmosphere, land and water. We have an individual connecting with their body, mind, and spiritual world. Countries connecting, continents connecting, regions connecting, homes connecting, bridges connecting, day to day human noises like dancing, crying, supplication, lovemaking, war, death, heaven and earth connecting humans. Connection is a slim condition of possibility without which humanity would tank. Connections are important to humans and the natural world, with human connections said to reduce health risks and improve physical welbeing and longevity. I need not emphaiszee how important it is for humans to have a good relationship with their environs as our poor relationship with earth has caused degradation of the environment and global warming which ultimately if its not rectified will end humanity and other living things on earth. There is no better compositional tool in art than the line which can connect plot to plot of an artwork. And in most of the paintings and drawings here I use the line as the composition tool and of course colour, as usual. It could be the swirling line, the curving line, the connecting line, the thick, thin, horizontal, dotted, vertical..."

And this is my artist statement
"My work takes the nature of interactive, collaborative and multidisciplinary. I work across several art fields, including among others literary (fictions, novels, essays poetry, play, short stories, songs...), musical (composition, singing, reciting, mbira, marimba, keyboards, hosho, ngoma and a little guitar...), and visual (drawings, paintings, photography, collages, mixed media, installation etc...) I am interested in connection, convergence, community and cooperation, following disparate sometimes disfigured experiences, seeing how they can come together or shy away from each other to create new wholes."

These are the ideas and issues the paintings and poetry in this collection are centered around, how us humans can connect with all sorts of worlds outside and inside us to ground ourselves on this stone called Earth.

MY LOVE

My love is like freedom,
Flying into flames!

My love is an act of faith,
Like moth's wings flying.

And nobody waits like I do,
For her teardrops to dry.

Which rolled out truths I could have denied.
And she's fooled me into believing I could wait.
Cursing myself for lost beauty slipping away.
But I have to hug my bundle like a honey pot.
Because she is all I have, all that I can't have.

But every sense in me is breaking out,
Like breath held against itself too long.
Whispering through the miles of my insides.
Smothering like bones melting inside a heart.
Like drops of flames through the ocean's waters.
Incommunicado, like you are telling it to nobody.

But underneath me lingers a subtle flame.
I behold you till I am speechless,
Holding you like a note from unfathomable ends.

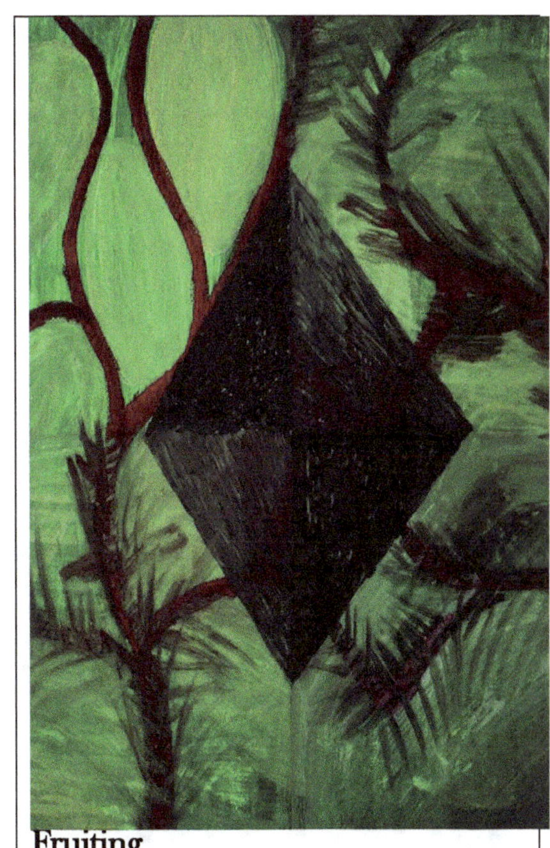

Fruiting

And I have to offer more in only three words.
The waters whose river we sense,
Uneasiness, falling like an angel, lost youth.
These people! They ask too much of us.
And this is what she smells of me.
The fears and frailties that make me love her.

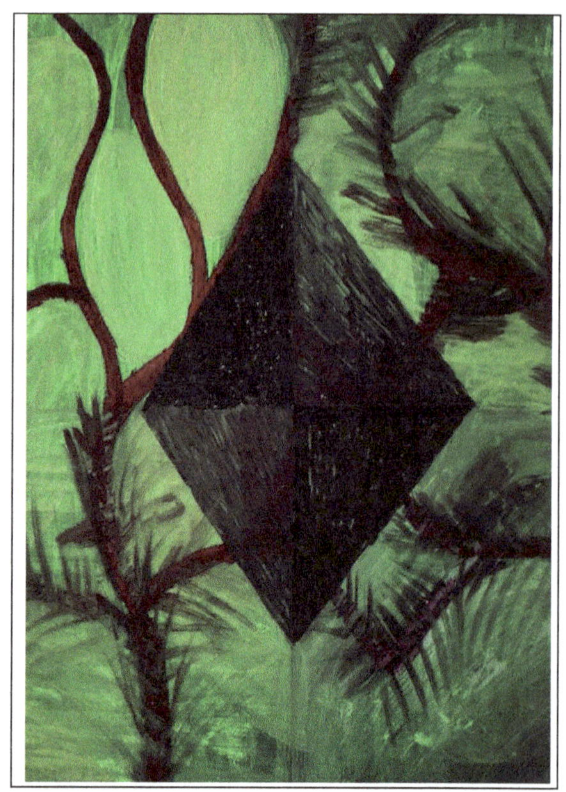

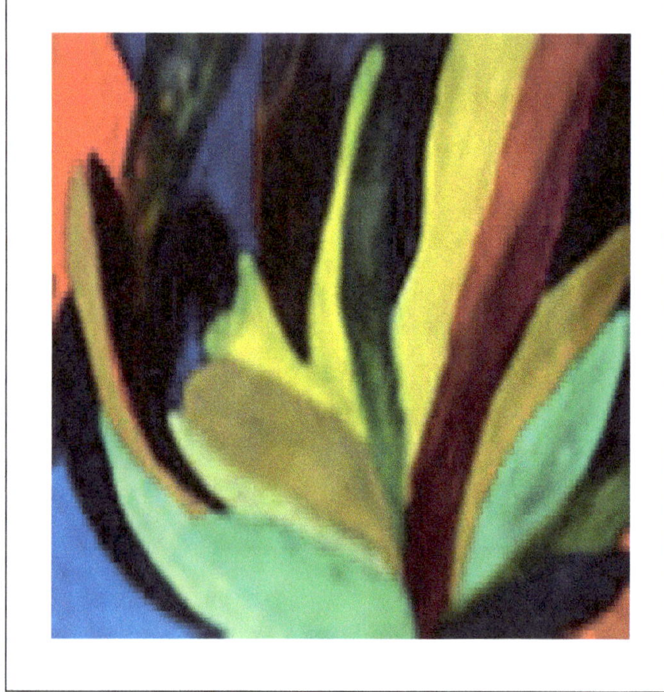

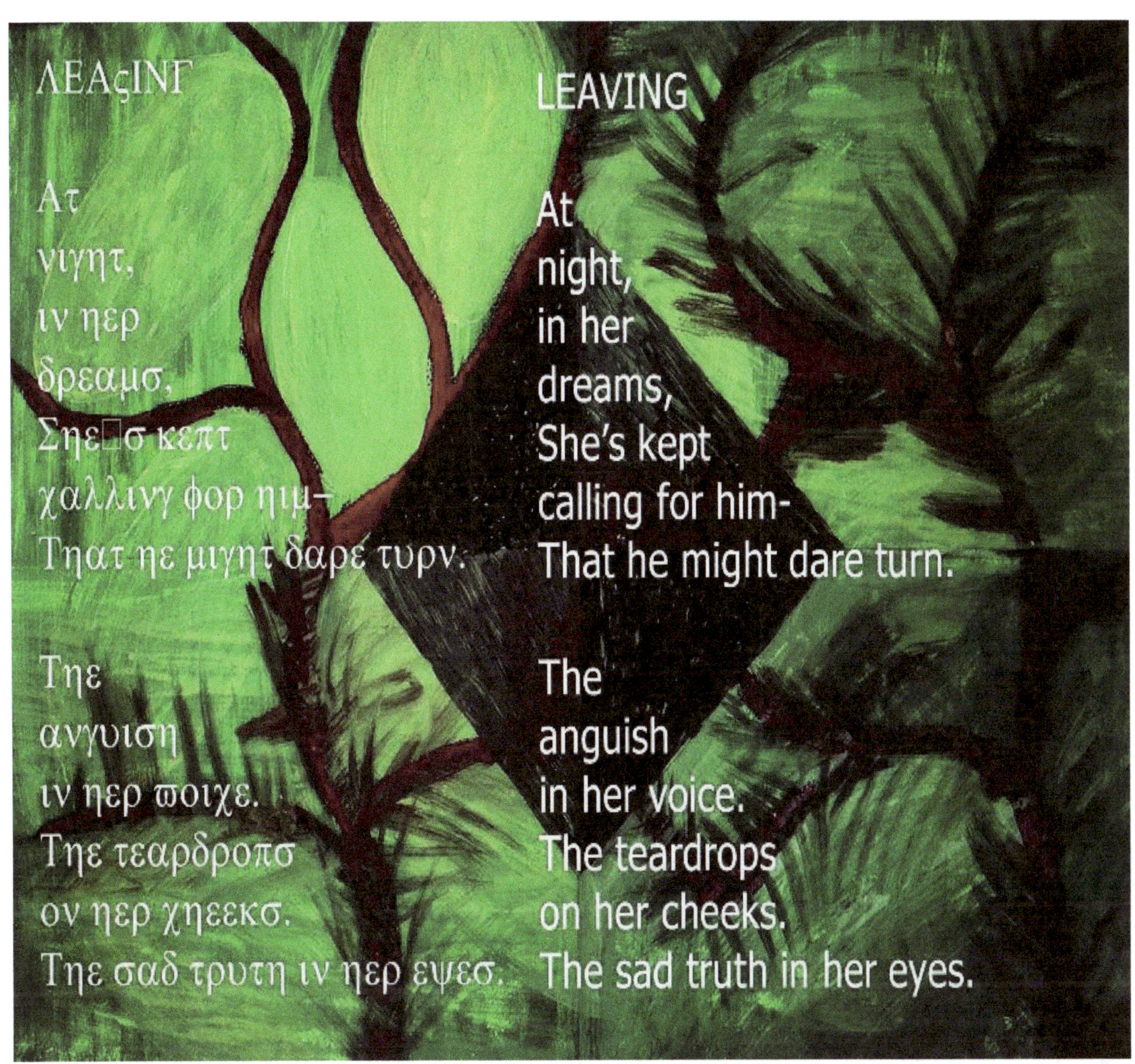
ΛΕΑςΙΝΓ

Ατ
νιγητ,
ιν ηερ
δρεαμσ,
Σηε□σ κεπτ
χαλλινγ φορ ημ-
Τηατ ηε μιγητ δαρε τυρν.

Τηε
ανγυιση
ιν ηερ ϖοιχε.
Τηε τεαρδροπσ
ον ηερ χηεεκσ.
Τηε σαδ τρυτη ιν ηερ εψεσ.

LEAVING

At
night,
in her
dreams,
She's kept
calling for him-
That he might dare turn.

The
anguish
in her voice.
The teardrops
on her cheeks.
The sad truth in her eyes.

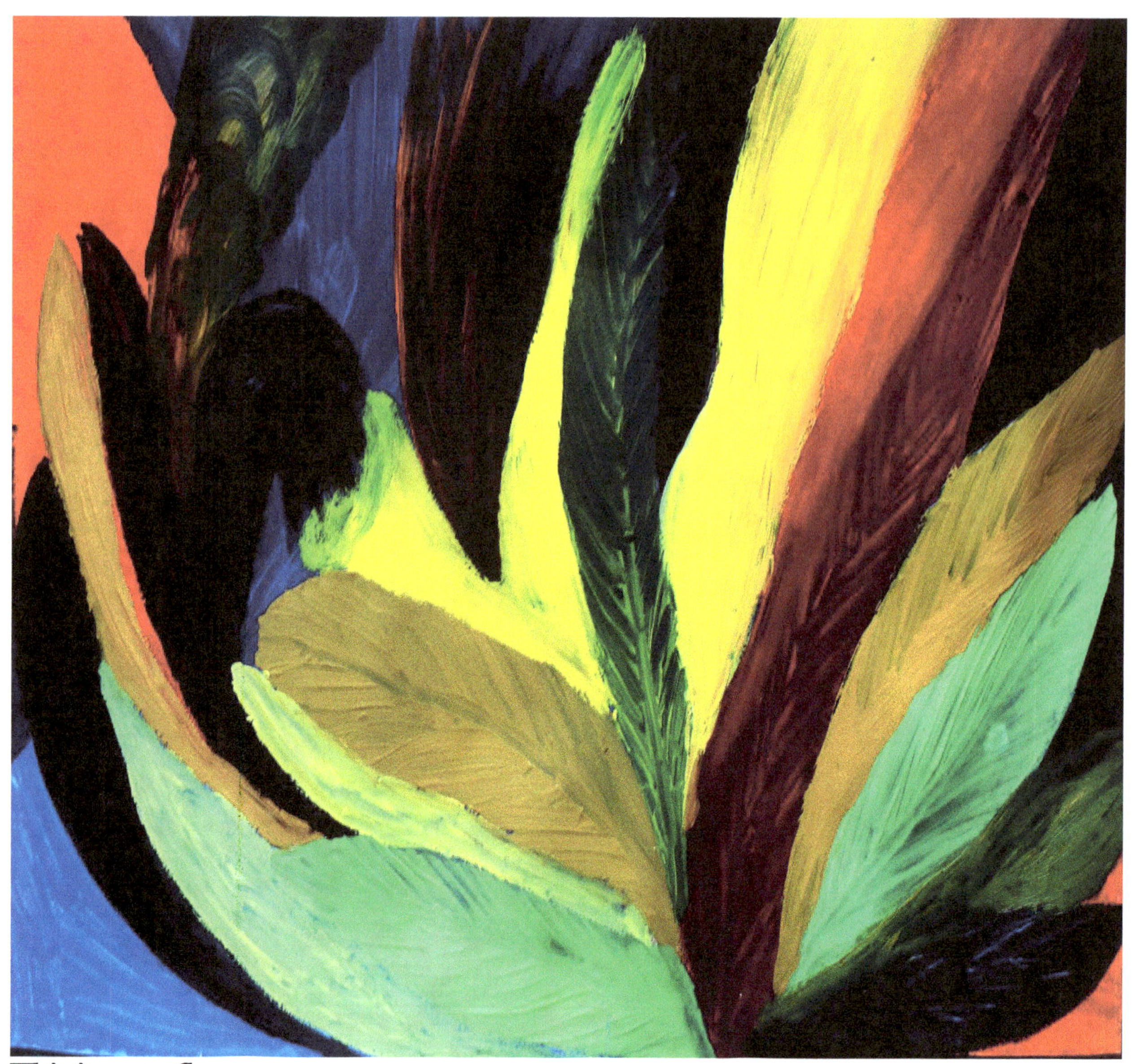

This is not a flower

WHY THE GIVING PROVES MINE ALONE?

Does it matter whether it is?
The mouth of the night
Or a lip of the night, extending
Into the day's fading light
Outside-in or inside-out
Night's light enveloping me
But love's aura, is a miraculous visitation!

She covers it, I wall it off, and then she hides it
Tell me, why the giving proves mine alone?
Like doubt to love to hate, hate to trust to dust
And it would begin to doubt to love to hate
And here is my love-mirror, a sweet see
Seeing sweetness through feelings and secret rites
And haven't I have wondered intoxicated
Through the shapes of a love, my love-mirror

love mirror

You stare and stare and it stares back at you. You laugh and it laughs back at you. You also know that whatever your image is. It is feeling the same things that you are also feeling. You aren't blocked. You aren't disturbed. You feel yourself entering into this image of yours. You are stuffing it up with all the things that you are feeling. You lock her in your arms. You close the world down. You fold time in. You also kill things from sheer curiosity here! You know you are also making an unconscious effort not to keep staring at this image. You can't close your inner eyes though. They keep staring at this image that is now deeply embedded inside you. She has become faith to you.

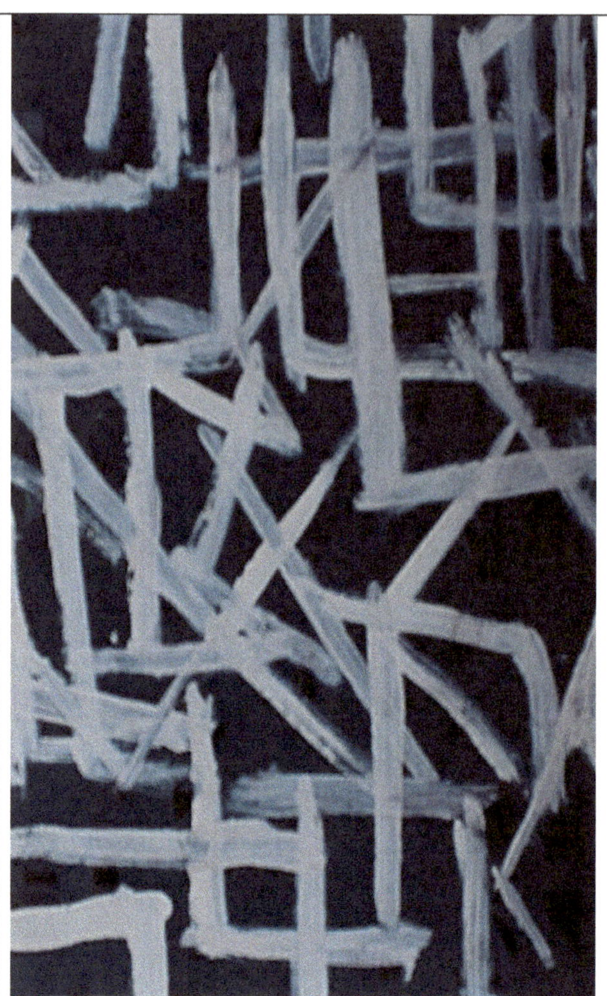

Their Meeting

naturally for Pauline

Hope still kindling dying desires
Like a breeze to a dying fire.
Absence fires too much of expectation.
Memories churns up the thoughts.
Feelings scatter all over.
Dump and blind!

Your last look, carefully cruel.
Permitting no compromise.
Suggesting no reversal, no promise
No tease, no condition.

And I myself thought,
That this love-
So keen yet so closed
Might spring by the slope.
Steep against its own ambitions?

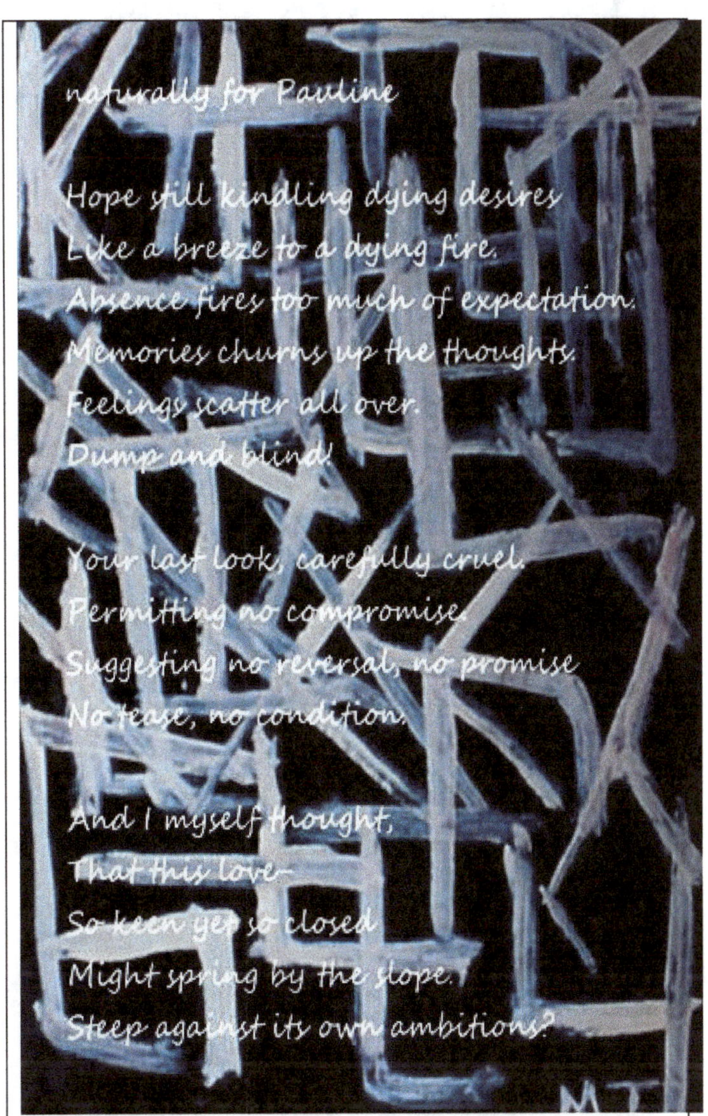

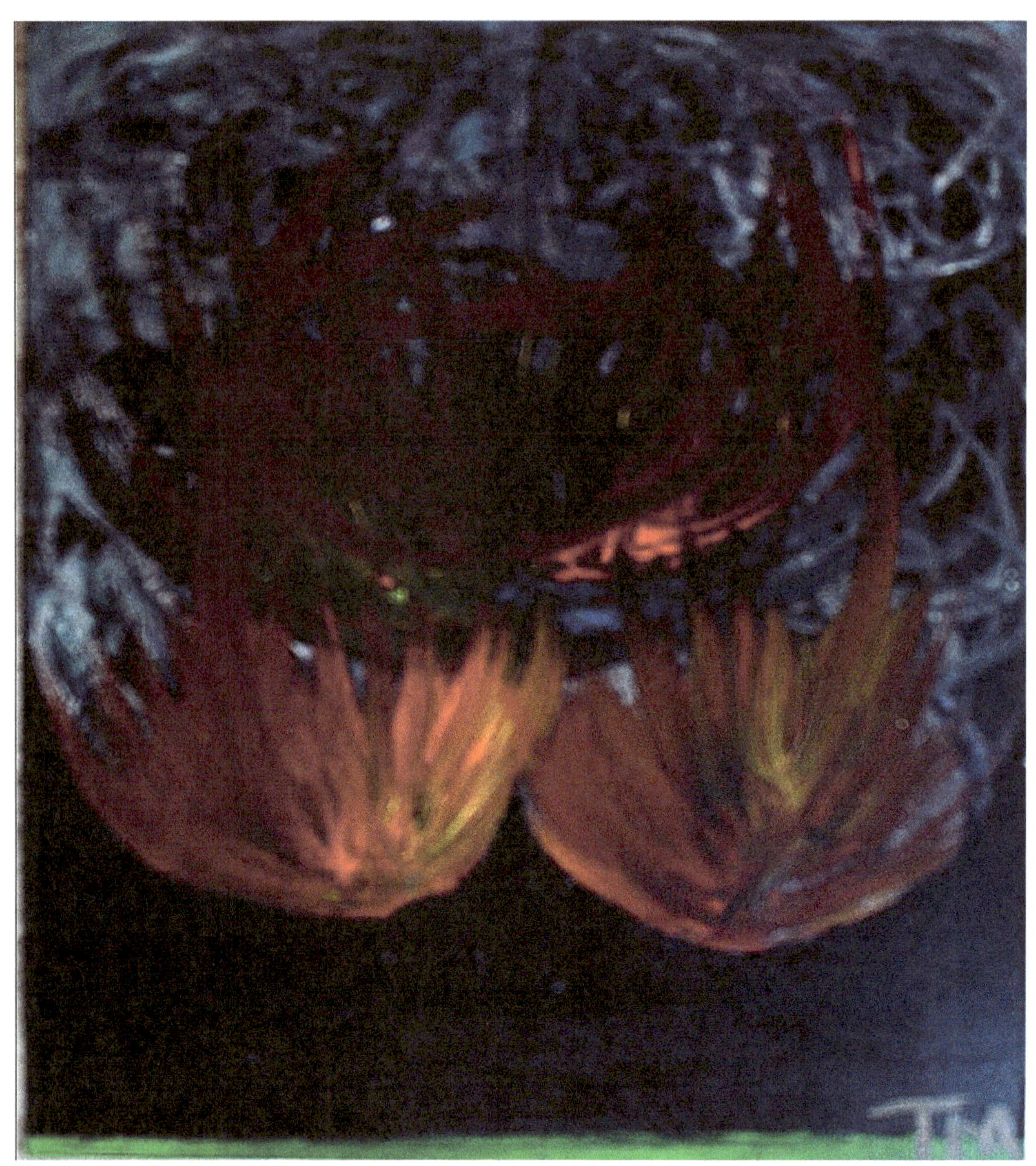

Pleasure domes

USE ME WELL

Women...weaponless women
Rushing at me on horses
Waving hands dripping blood.

The river tumbling in the distant
In a village mud-hut
And I like this view
But not the furnishings.

Feelings inviting self-indulgence
That's how I compose my love
A peculiar design for love.

I am pregnant with my love
And I will die giving birth to it
How so, like a woman.

Part of my love dwells underneath
That part reacts
And she is that part within me.

She knows me so well
Like a woman knows her man
But I despair of her
Ever understanding me.

She so loves me...

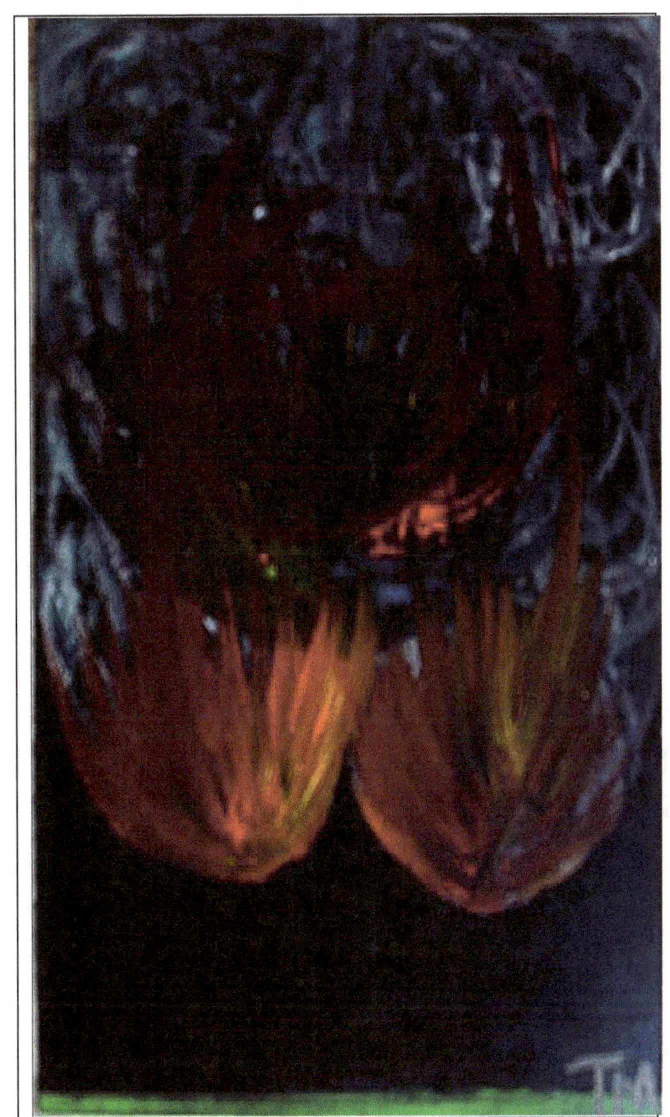

Without knowing, thinking
What is it to be her?
She has no wherewithal of

She is like shouted words
I spoke them
But no one heard them
Perhaps someone would hear them
Silence is loved by silence!

She uses love as a persuader
Even when she spites me
And use me well...
For I cherish her

Boldness is distraction
Walking in the open
Is not love's tradition
It is not a word for men

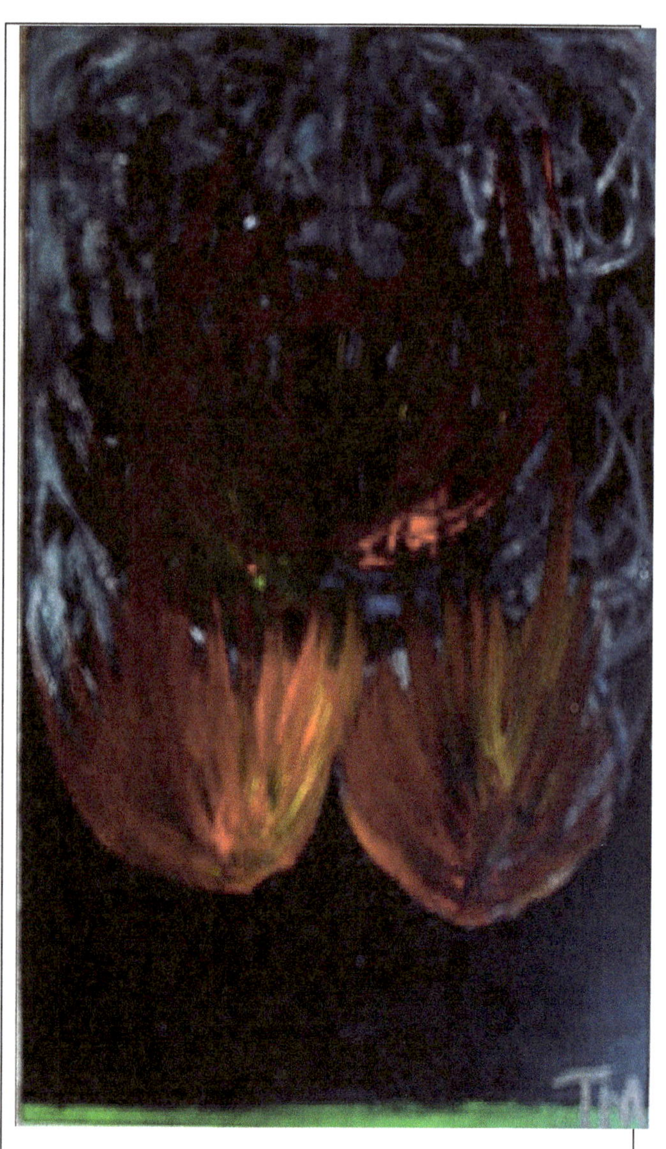

A JOY HERE...

The summer's rains soaking
Centuries walking
Like love of creation
Up and down this terrain
The terrain of our own choice

Continuously generating
Security and comfort
And bestowing life to this story
A story of our own creation

A joy here, impelling the essences
And a sorrow there
And in between
The sun is generously shinning
And melting edges of difference
And dissipating indifferences

Star to star on our path we are
To a chosen destiny of purpose
And like autumn's showers towering
Autumn's love is lifting above
A glowing peak seen
So long as it takes an eye

Unafraid of what fate's influences

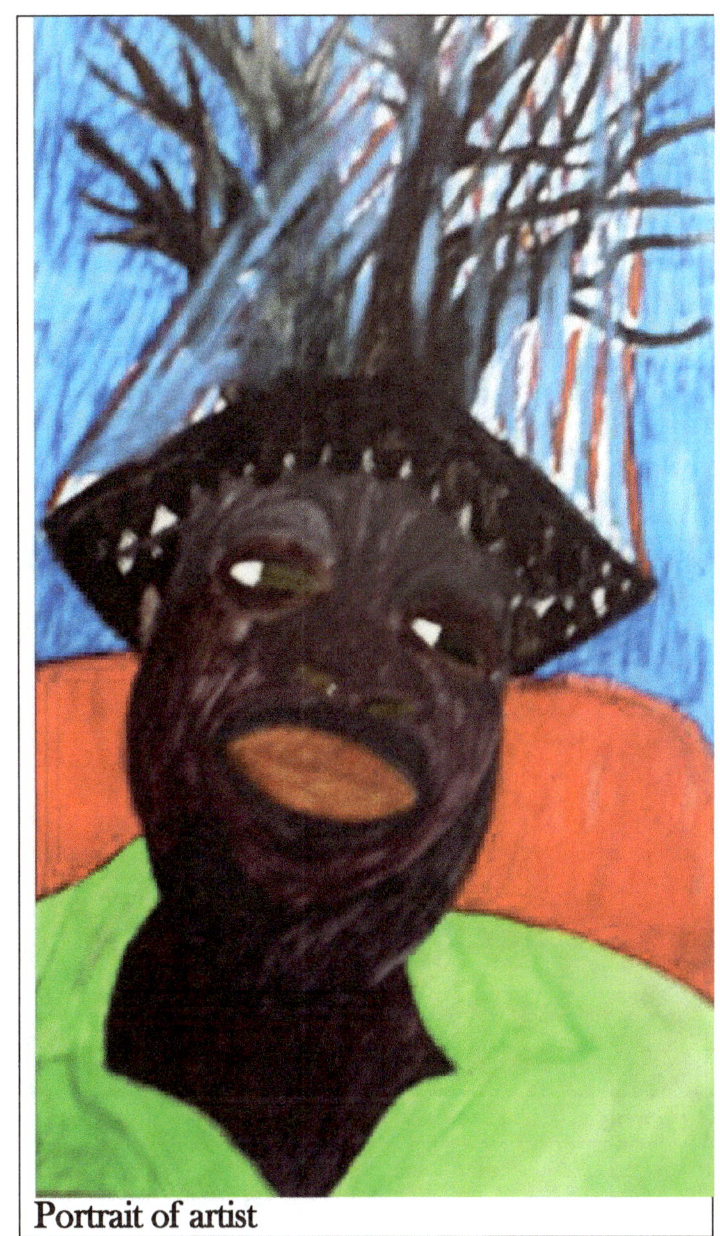

Portrait of artist

Might dare find in us, for
None of these are our concerns
But we find
In these lingering restrictions
A leisurely fiction

That reveals realities
Mapping our footfalls
And fulfilling our promises
Impelling the essences of our intents

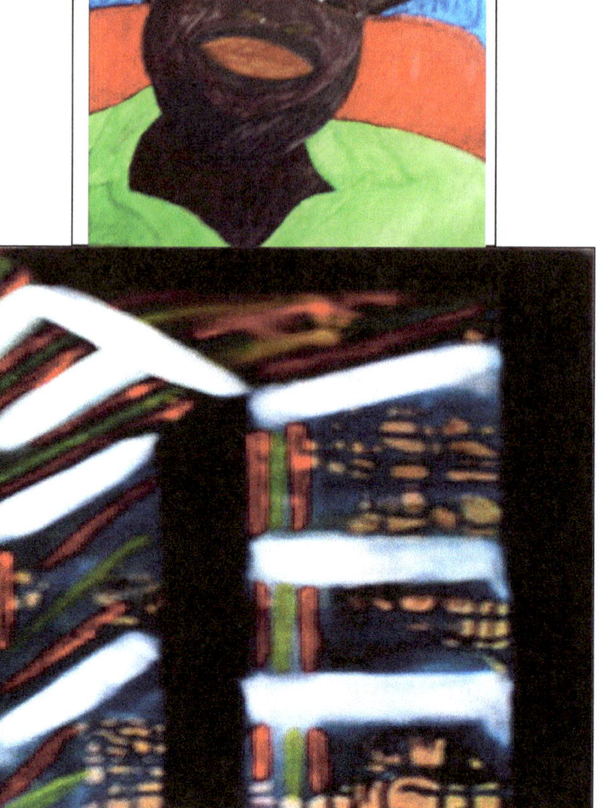

Home

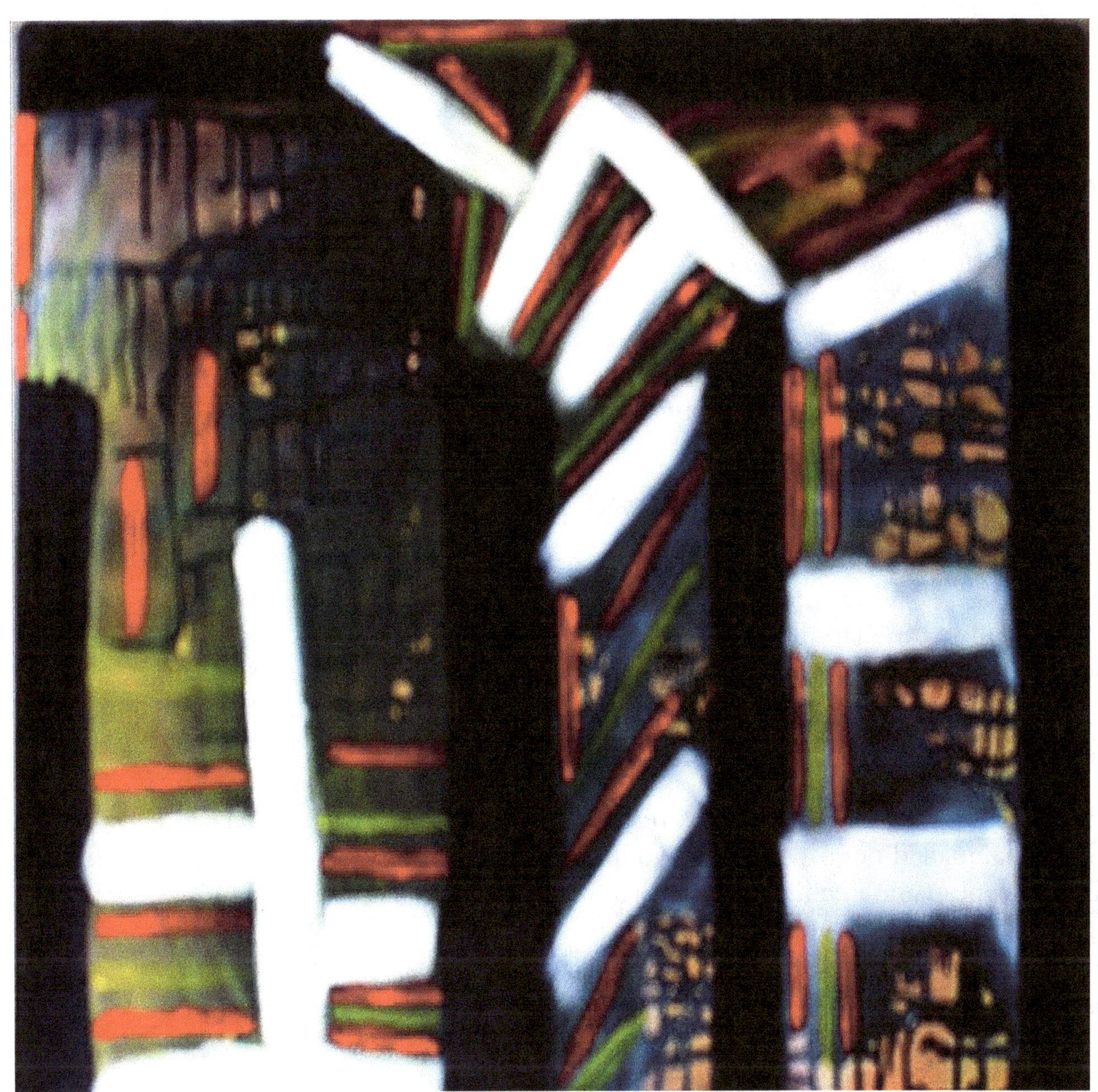

CALLING FOR YOU

everyday that we live
we throw pebbles into the pool
and the pebbles create ripples
someday the ripples would meet.

you say you are leaving me today. we are sixteen, young and immature. coz in our hearts we know we have to let go. in my heart i know, i can't let you go. in your heart you know, we never meant to be. in our hearts we know, we have to marry others

but our safety net is
that someday
i would come for you

can i glimpse the map that's sending you away. can i feel the price you are paying now. can't delay you, to help me escape. our hearts touches the pure silence between us. could only think of you, on and off over the years. and she left me after thirty years together. and i knew it was time to call for you

goggled your name on the net, the rest is history. left Phoenix Arizona for Toowoomba Australia. mailed out my love to the address of your heart. Rod Stewart says the first cut is the deepest. and i believe its true, that we belong together

this is my heart's call
that today
that's calling for you

and at all times respect your heart's potential. by following your path through your heart. step strongly into your eternal sunset. for a push can bring us out of our calling. in a lifetime contrived by time. the mountain is calling us to its peak again. and our calling becomes another calling. another calling, and another calling...calling for you.

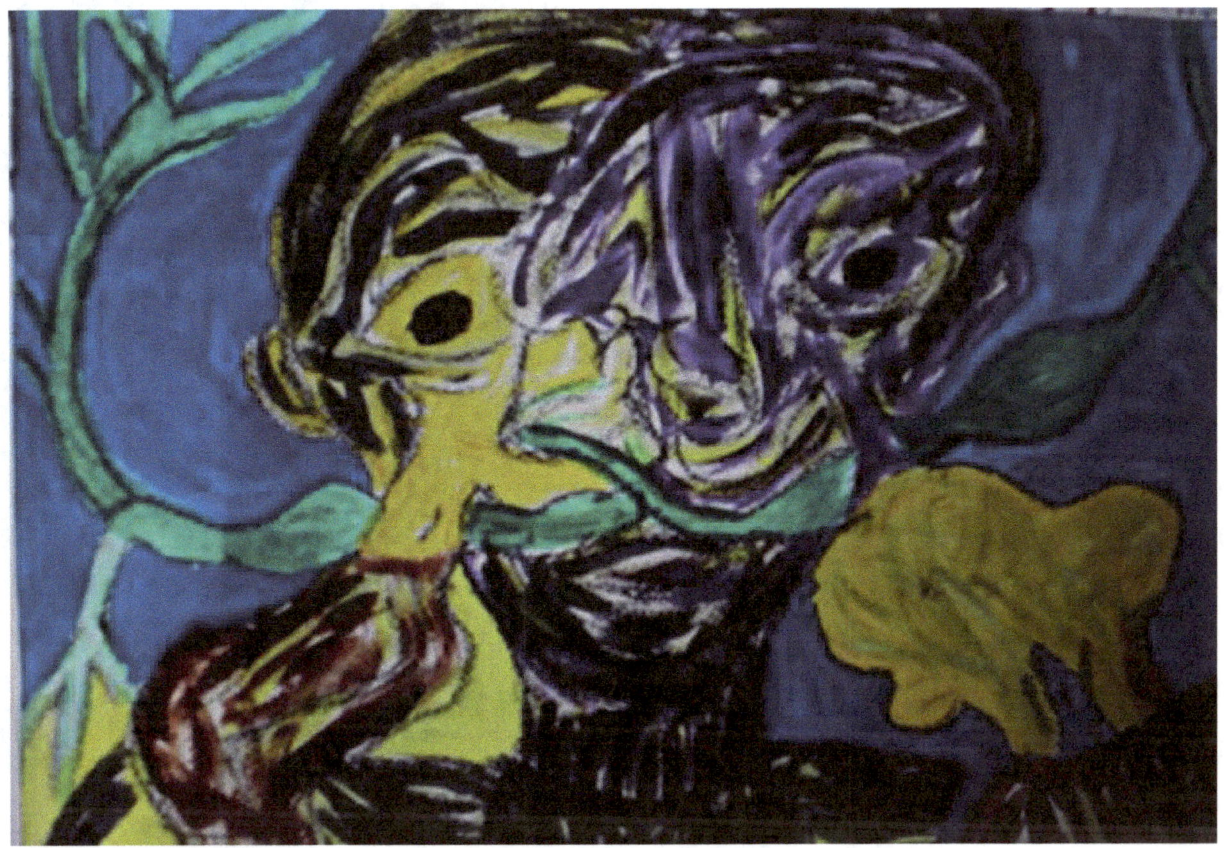

When I call your name

I AM POISONED

My body is poisoned with foreign waters.
The shadow dances of Rand's waters,
And those logged words.

My mind has surrendered to fears,
Sans weighted fears-
And thoughts of doom.
Sinking inside of myself.

My consciousness is filled with images-
Of sun-drenched days,
In the streets of Harare.
If not of all those guilty acts?

My only consolation is that,
One day I shall return back for you.
But I doubt that you-
Would want me-
This changed?

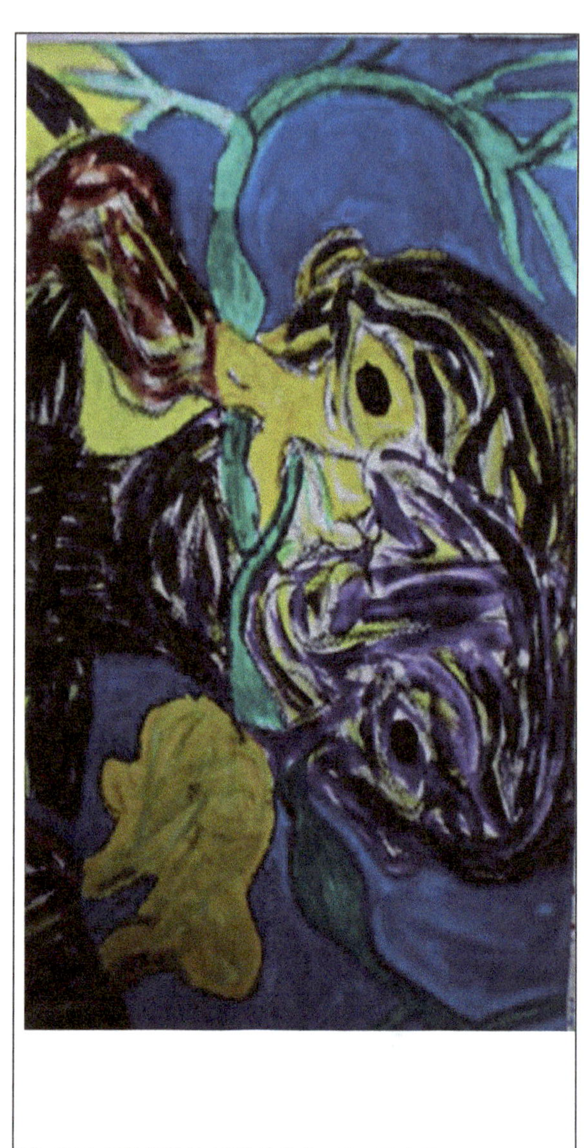

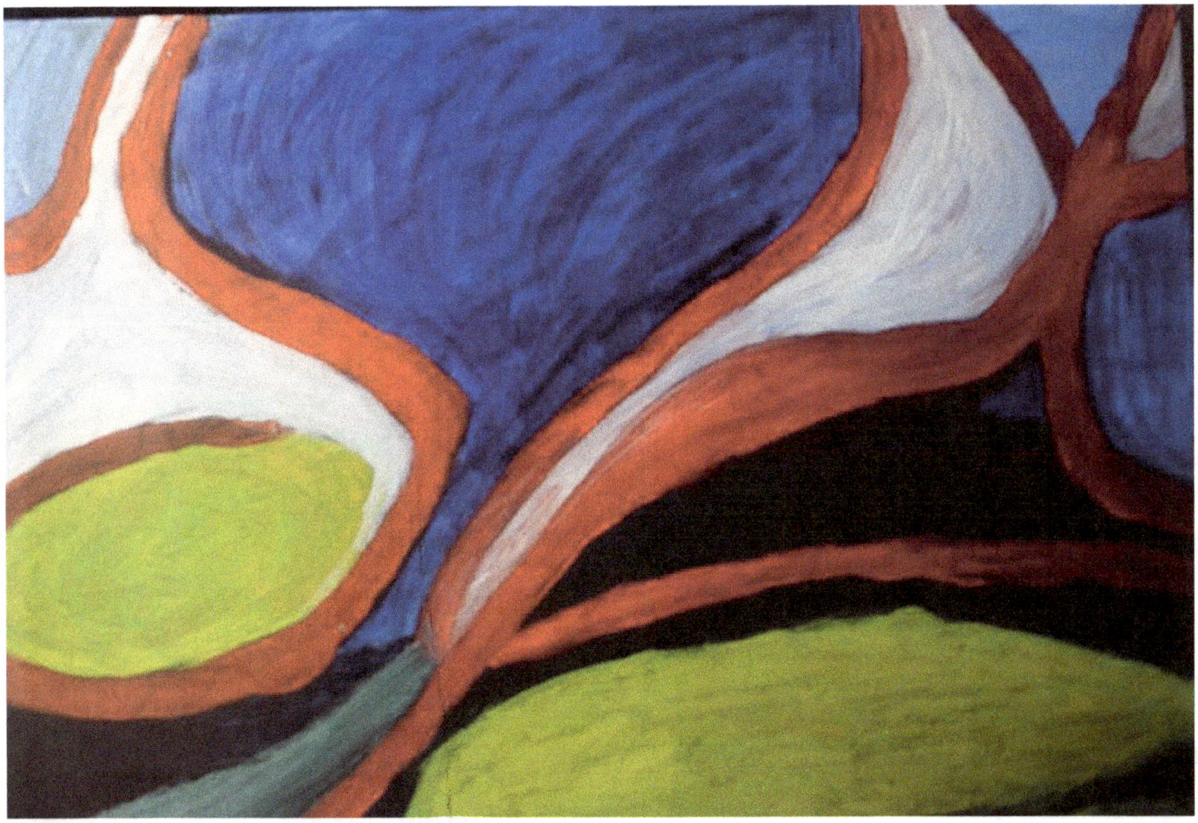

Womb

WHO WOULD PLAY THE HUSBAND?

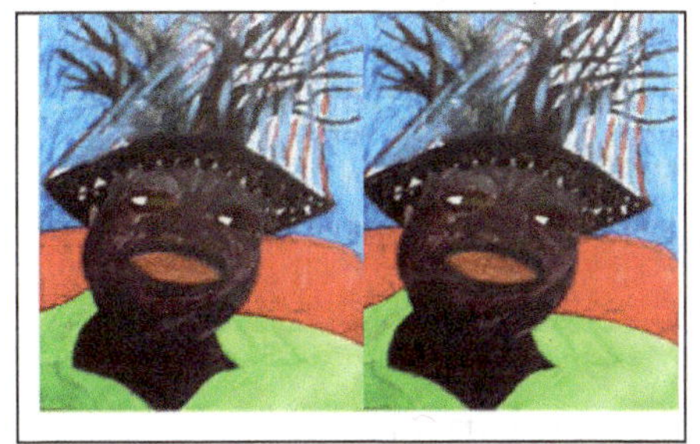

I don't usually suffer love gladly
So I practice the art of concealing love
When revealing it could be harmful
And it explains all these empty words

Nothing can be done about,
The inescapable mass of her body
Except to keep herself in the shadows
And she often prefers these deep waters
Throwing most of the light on me
Like playing a fish on a line

I always feel her restrained passions
And know my deepest fears
The problem of love is inevitably;
Who would play the husband?
And my immediate problem is
If she would require children;
I would choose the father

I can sense the man in me
The man who might have been
I am possessed of certain excitements
Not available to most others
Intelligence built upon sensitivity
But she is not sure of my abilities

Perhaps she would be truthful
Perhaps she would answer-
The odd expression in her eyes
And I wish this image in her eyes
Would reproduce me
Some bizarre form of a love?

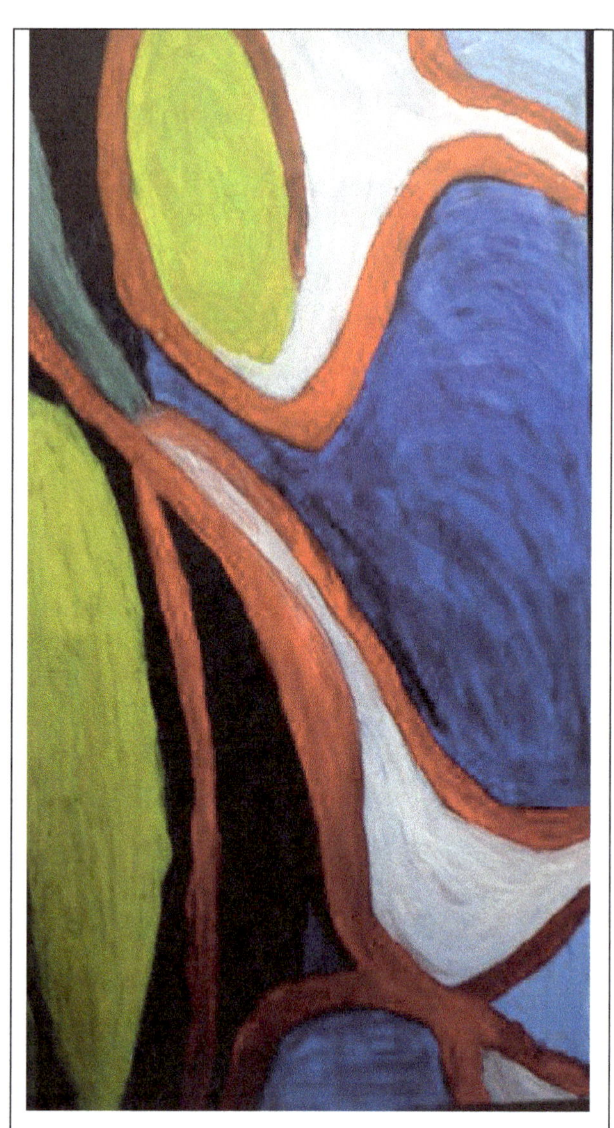

MAYBE

Maybe
this poem will leave me
Chastened in my heart.
Maybe this ditty will leave me
With a crushed leaf of a desire.
Like a chilled Zombie with its ditties
Elegizing about the lost sun
By the warmy sun-brushed stone.

Maybe
I will never reach home again.
Maybe I will never know her again.
Extend retract, her sweet anger
Tongue-drew welts inside my heart.
And her beauty, a riot of spreading bruise.

Maybe
the still painful wind inside me
Will freshen and re-direct, away
Her bundled violence out of my heart.
And I will hang-on tight to this slope
Wallowing in her wake!

Maybe
someday I will totally expose myself
To the naked penetrating touch

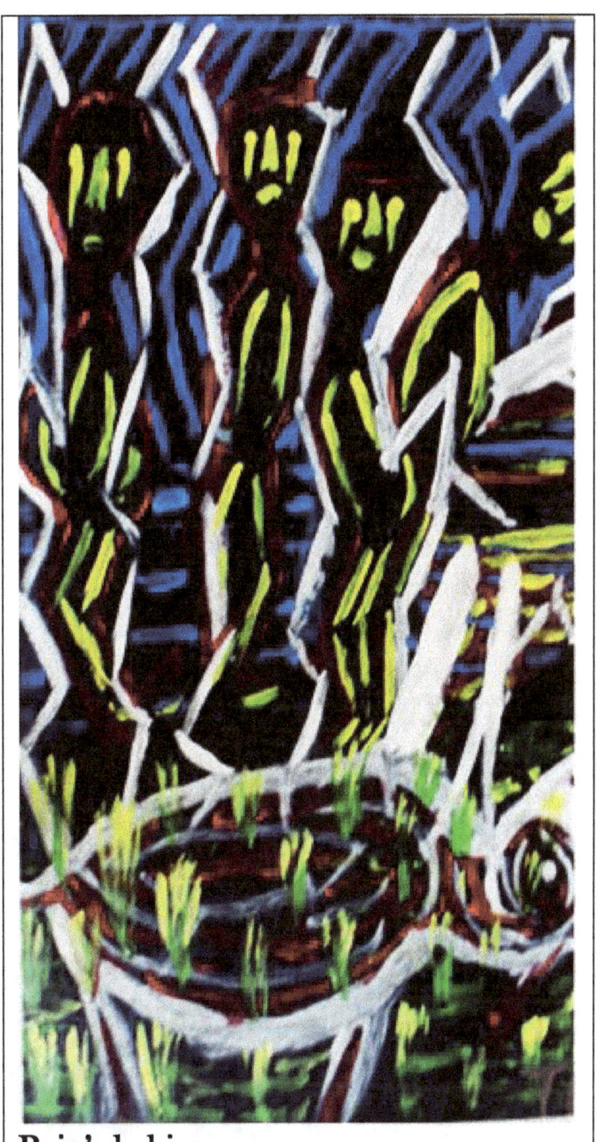

Rain's babies

Of my feelings for her.
Freezing every iota in my heart
To a sure hardening of the core.
Maybe some day I will,
with my heart frozen
Beam with light that has failed to shine.

Maybe
my frozen heart will chain to life again
Splitting into screams,
like the spring's
Laugh lines unfurling in the rains!
Each drop, a tiny cataract cooling me
Whilst I dance in circles and smile
With a new secret.

Maybe
my heart will die with grace
To re-enter love again and now
Curse with an unacquired knowledge.

I CANNOT CRY

I respect her so much,
to ague with her.
And I cannot cry-
For tears always have
intentions.

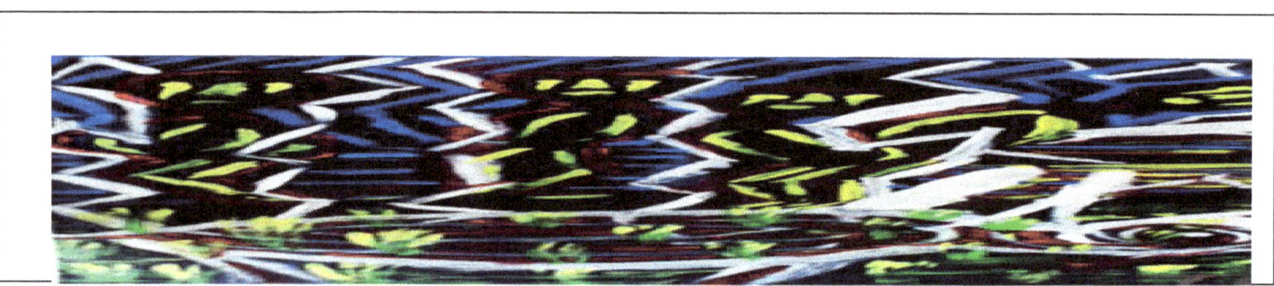

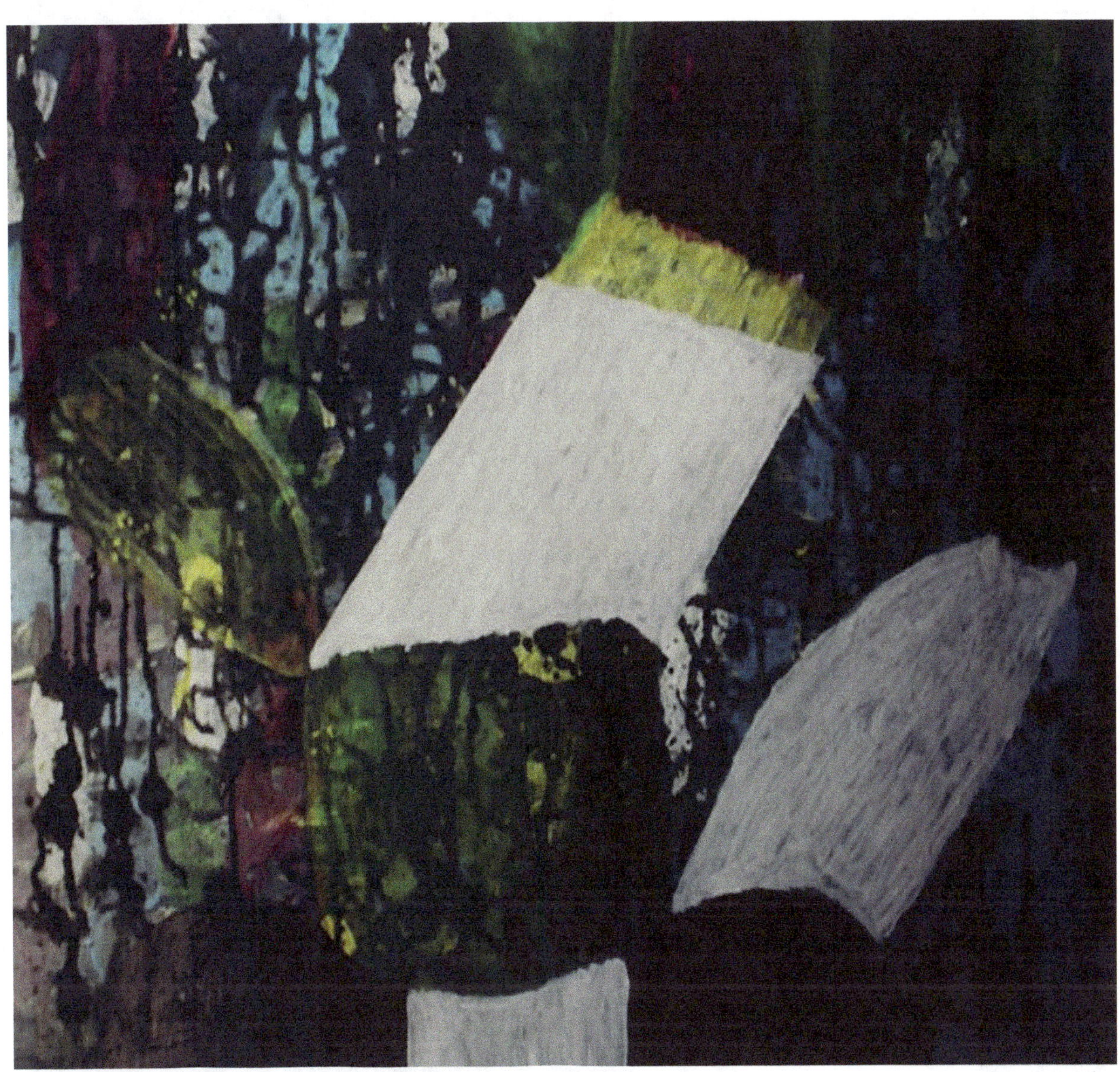
The walking dead

LOVE CAN BE

The last
of the sun's light-
gilding the lone bird's,
flighty feathers.

Women
whirling before-
an inner eye, heads thrown,
in an ancient movement.

Straggling
across long-dead...
faces, the mating dance,
of African women

Like bees
returning often-
to their hives,
our caves are still there.

And love
can be a lonely-
estate, of wounded seams,
and tarnished dreams.

With messages
Written on the spray,

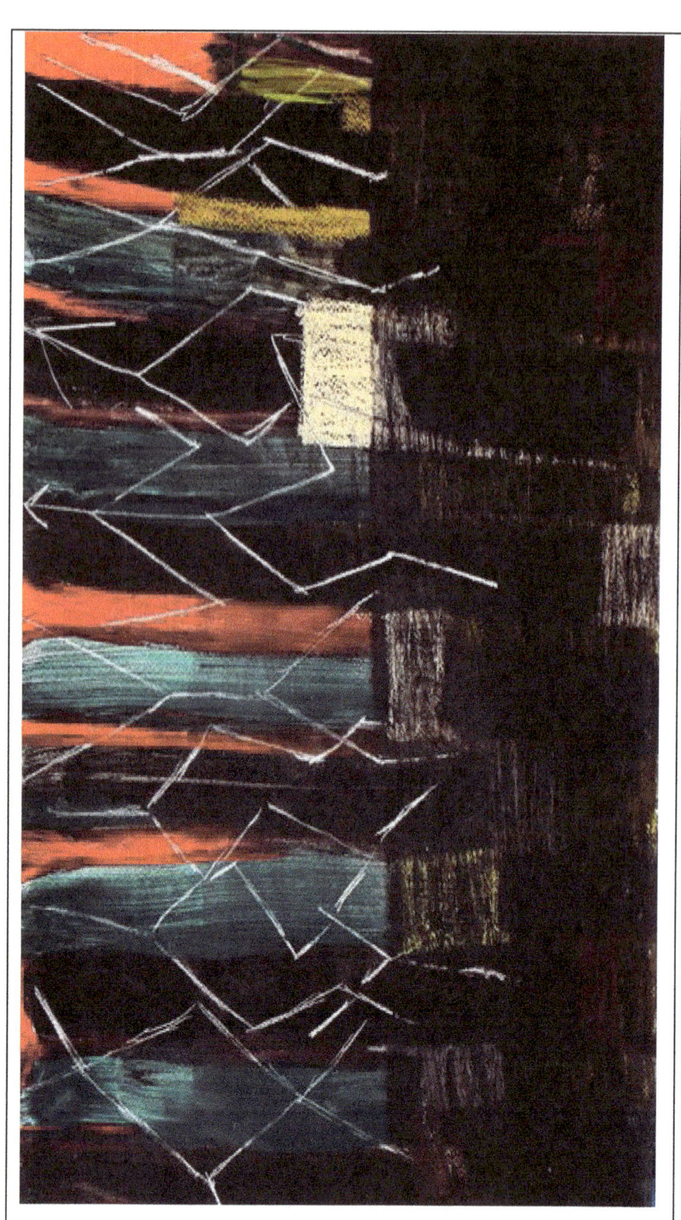

of huge, torrentials,
of rains.

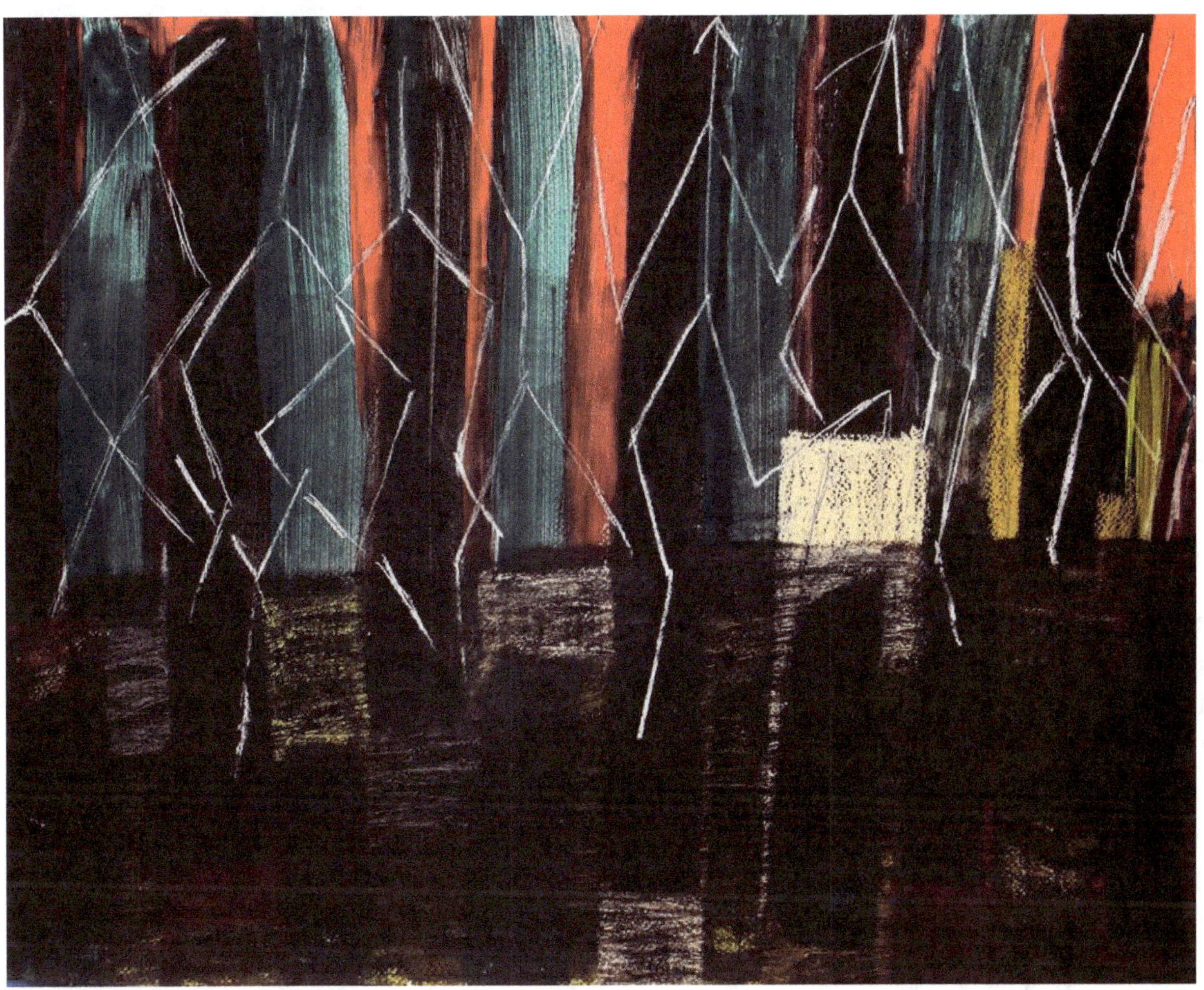

Dancing

PLAYING TO LOVE'S GALLERY

The wind makes a humming sound
  as the wind stirs the dust,
    conveying these messages.
      Perhaps amusing messages
        or even lovely thoughts, touching...

Her nearness into my heart
and could she really get into my heart
without prior warning?
Accelerating arrangements!

Making it as-soon-as-possible a thing,
    her love-focusing dishes are an essential love-trap
        with destined to occur colours
          that even the victim can never reject.

She possesses her own horns,
the fluttering horns that whispers
into the air at nightfall.
And I sense a waiting captivity.

Something has to be spoken
  and she would respond from the wells
    of what time has done to her.
      I am courting her and I can sense into her soul
        and make her do things
          that she couldn't have done on her own

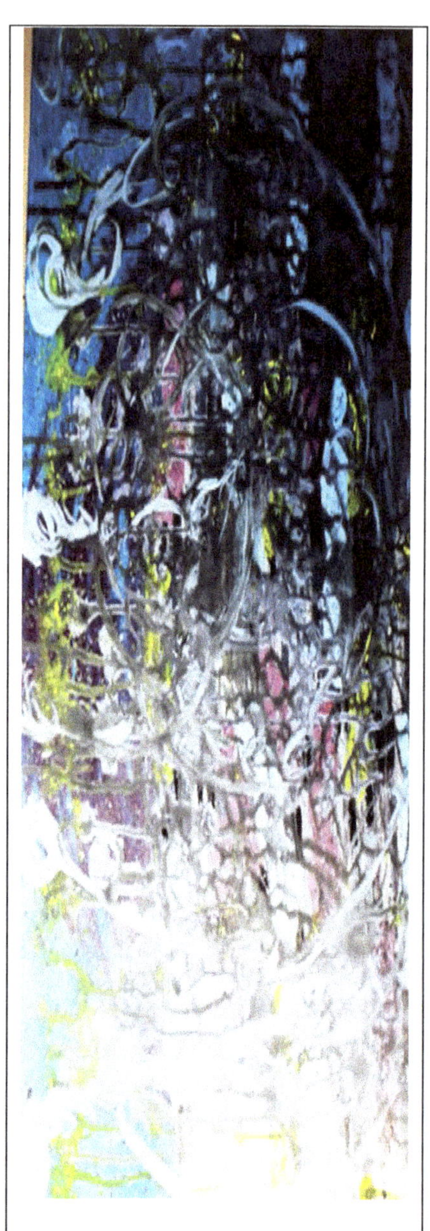

Yet, I cannot hurt her because I know
it's different with her but I don't know
what to do with her.
I only wish if she had not been here with me
then she would never have been mine.

And she would if she could
  but she cannot,
   kill herself!
     Playing to love's gallery is a re-agent
      that reveals more than she wants to show

I love her so much that I have rationed my visits,
by always making a long list of love's rituals
that have to be broken and be mend
for me to play and pretend
that I possess no cares

But into the distant layers of my heart,
  voices far into the deeper chambers of my heart
    which no one else knows of and hears
     are beating against a stone,
       a thumping sound in my heart.

And several other stones are tumbling
from my inner walls,
breaching barriers that locked my soul

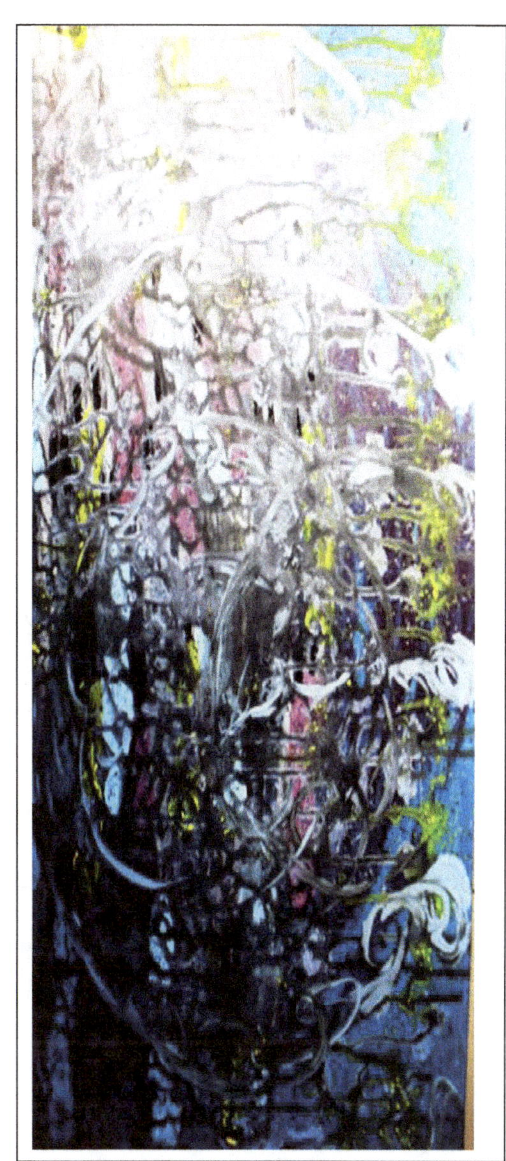

Loving someone is a thing
that you would do alone by finding a stranger
in your own heart and touching them
like touching light feels like touching
a world inside of itself.

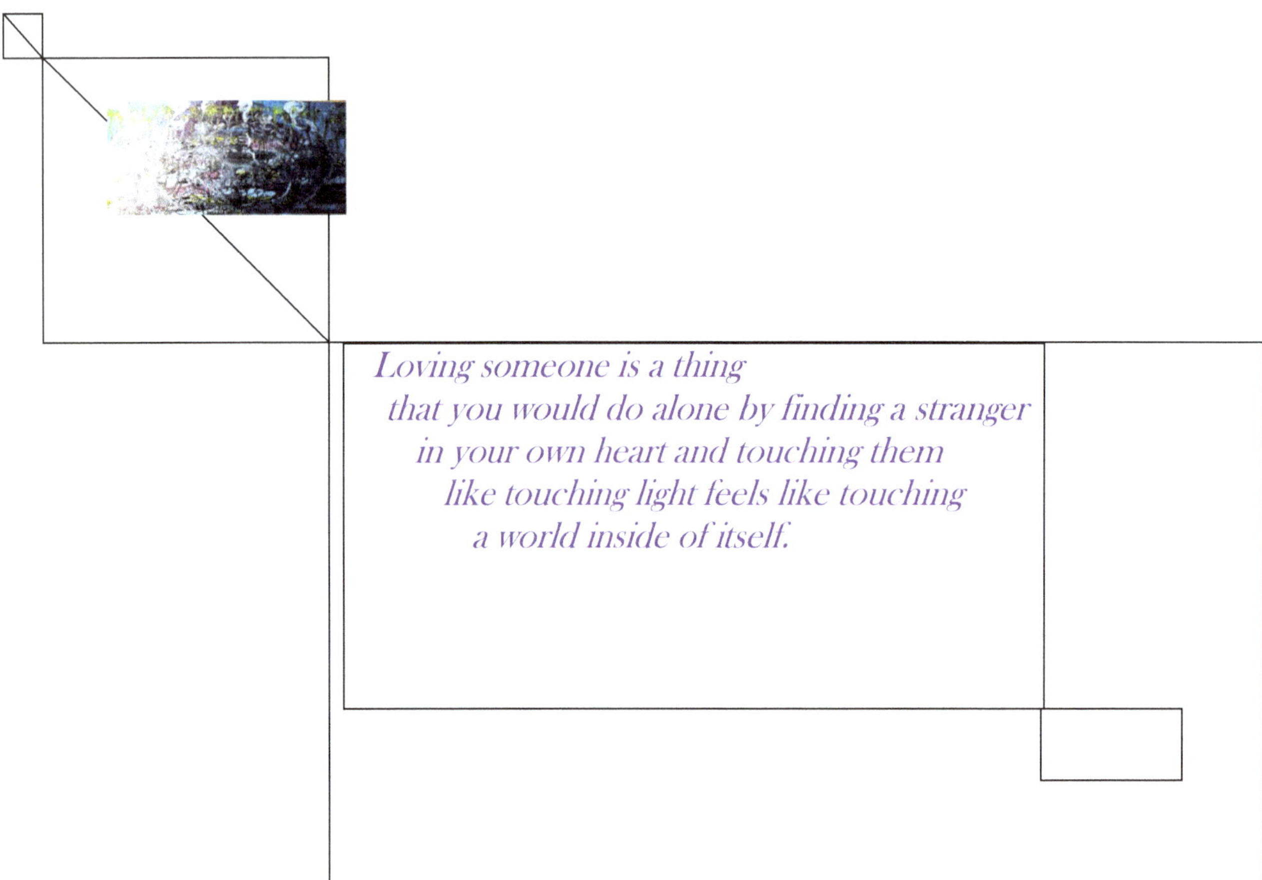

Loving someone is a thing
that you would do alone by finding a stranger
in your own heart and touching them
like touching light feels like touching
a world inside of itself.

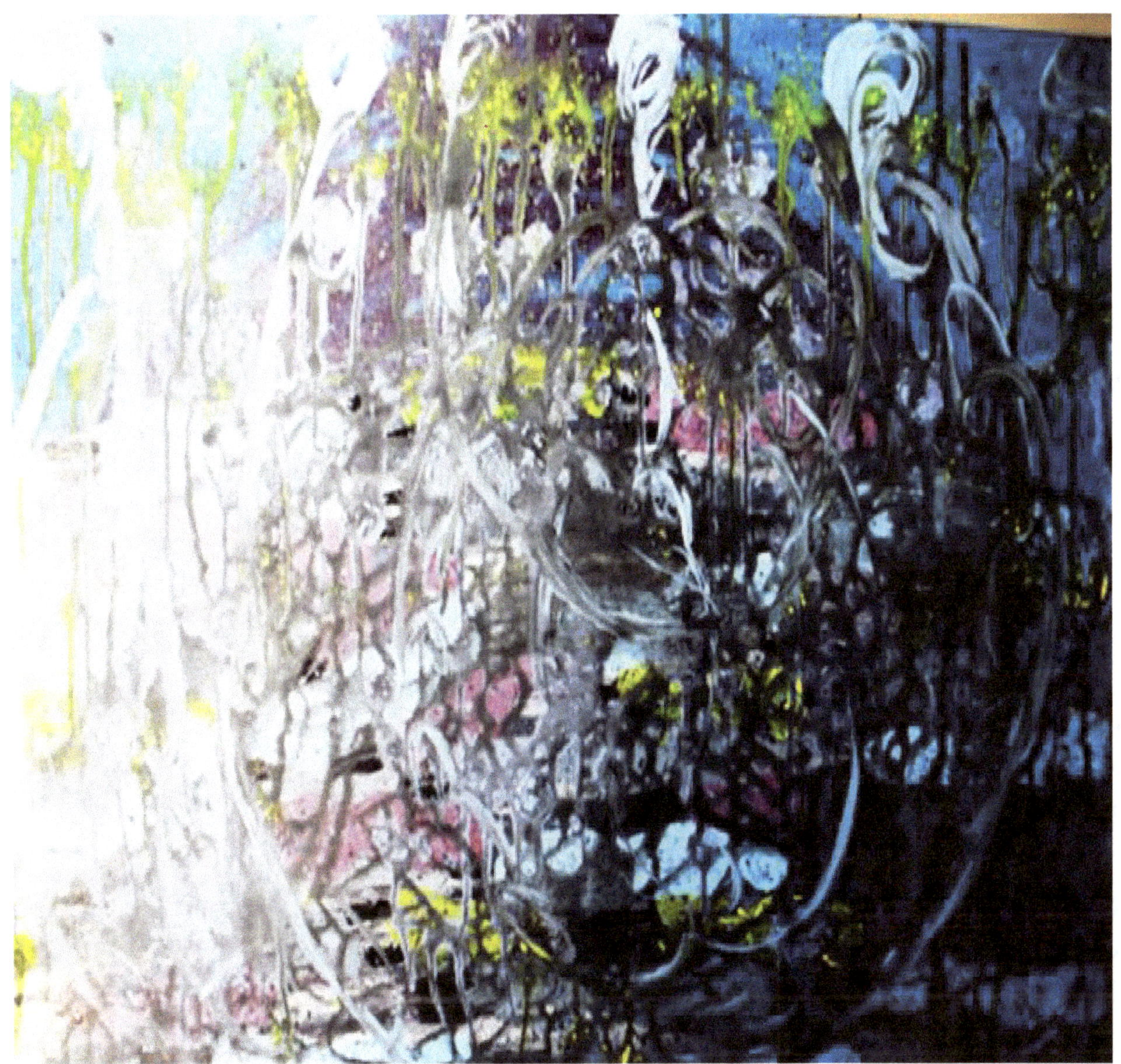

The flower of the dead

VOICES FROM WITHIN US

Life...laughter and joy
Are the only truths
Trapped within words
Love comes into our lives
Like vagrant eddies
Colouring the winds
But its spirit dims
Disappears, and is gone
Have we time?
They wanted to be with us
Look, at the love
Lying longingly untapped
Love big as the sky, open
Like a way of revenge
Held back as punishment
The price you will pay
You will pay in full
To dole it as a reward
Like sunshine on trampled grass
Someone is begging us
To be there now
To share and care
In each other's arms
Do we perceive their voices?

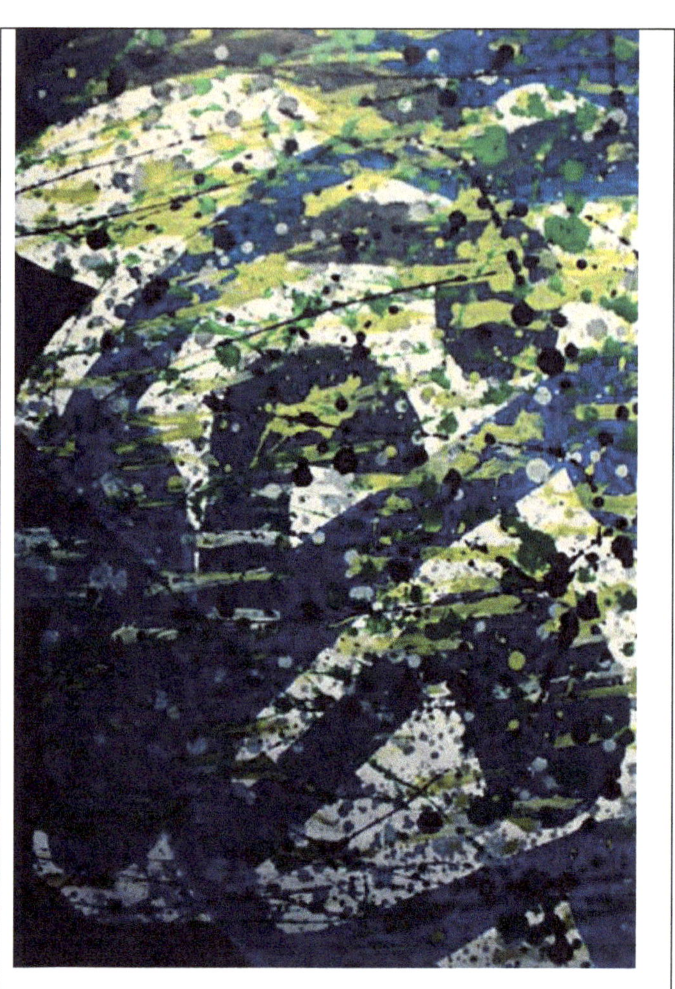

Deep within us
Like first shelvings, of
A narrow single of a beach
And as we strive
On our way beyond
All these ancient measures
True would be the happiness
Of understanding each other
No matter what content
To me that's what counts

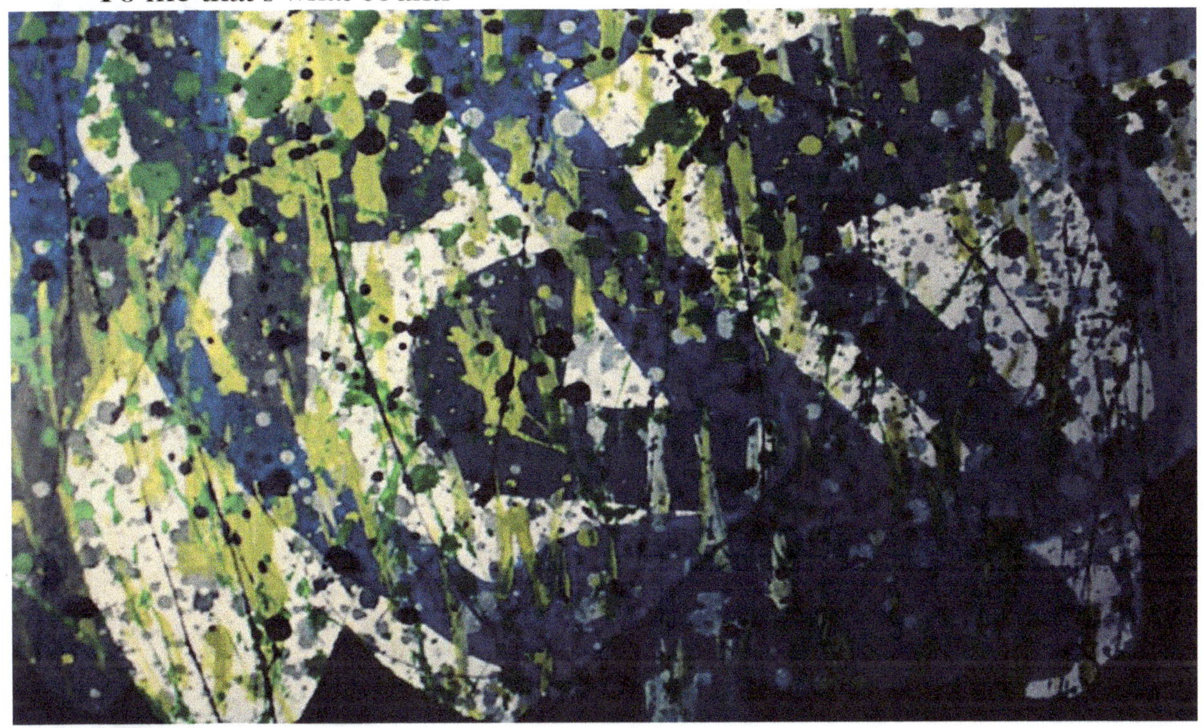

Love big as sky

love

This is a name you have forgotten. But its memory still lingers in your mind. Colours of this name are bursting into touch. Every touch of her hands is an endless rehearsal. You feel her hands on you even when she is not there with you. It is your skin. The biggest organ of your body! It is so alive like a pointillist painting: that from far away looks so seamless. Your desire for her is an endless landscape of alpha. You remember the memories of moulting into this relationship. A photo-tactic tongue ebbing away. Thoughts of her keep swimming up your mind. An insistent fish. Unseen insects across your skin. In the black holes of your mind. You remember the shacking off of final traces. In the wind of your last kisses with Patricia. You also have discovered that this love is now your accomplished existences. Bursting through in lyrical bubbles. Singing of a re-echoing the world of flooding gaps. It is a song that has lulled you to a sleep. It is an open sky. The rains are falling down on you. You let them rain down on you, boy! So this love of yours has survived. The face of man in what is divine?

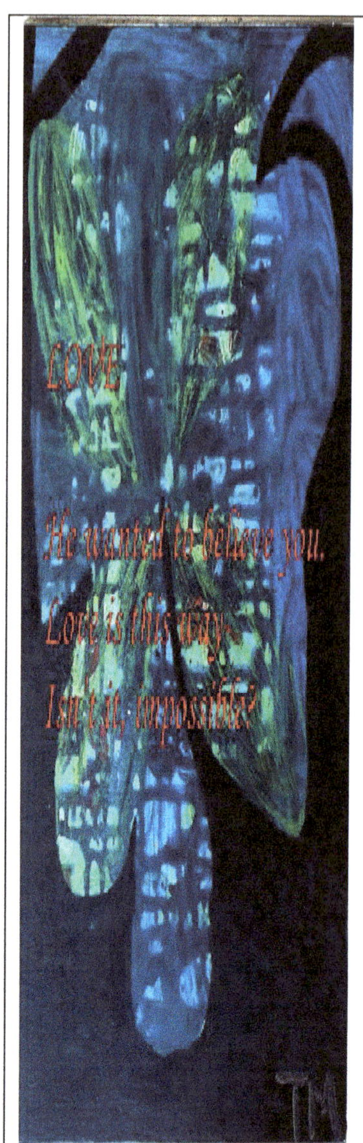

Butterflies dancing

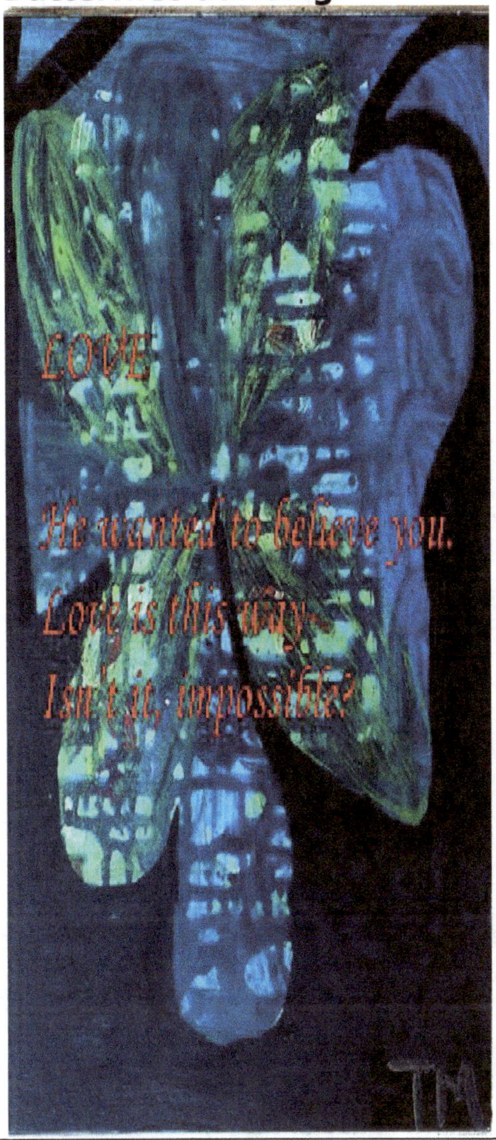

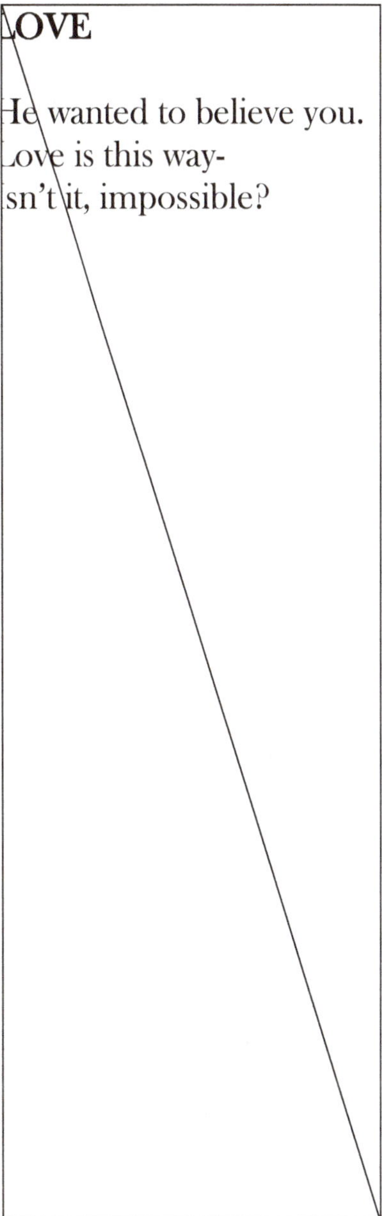

LOVE

He wanted to believe you.
Love is this way-
Isn't it, impossible?

LIKE A FABRIC TORN

A care within which
Love might appear
It is a link to love
On several levels
And our particular openness
Fills us with warmth

And the sun listens to
Easy laughter
On top of the mountains
In a warm autumn sky

Soft winds alive
With millions of
Lasting, sweeping
Love's breaths
Flowering feeling into emotions

Stars are stepping stones
To dreams as clear
And as deep denied
As water

Like the wishful
Drying sounds of the clothes

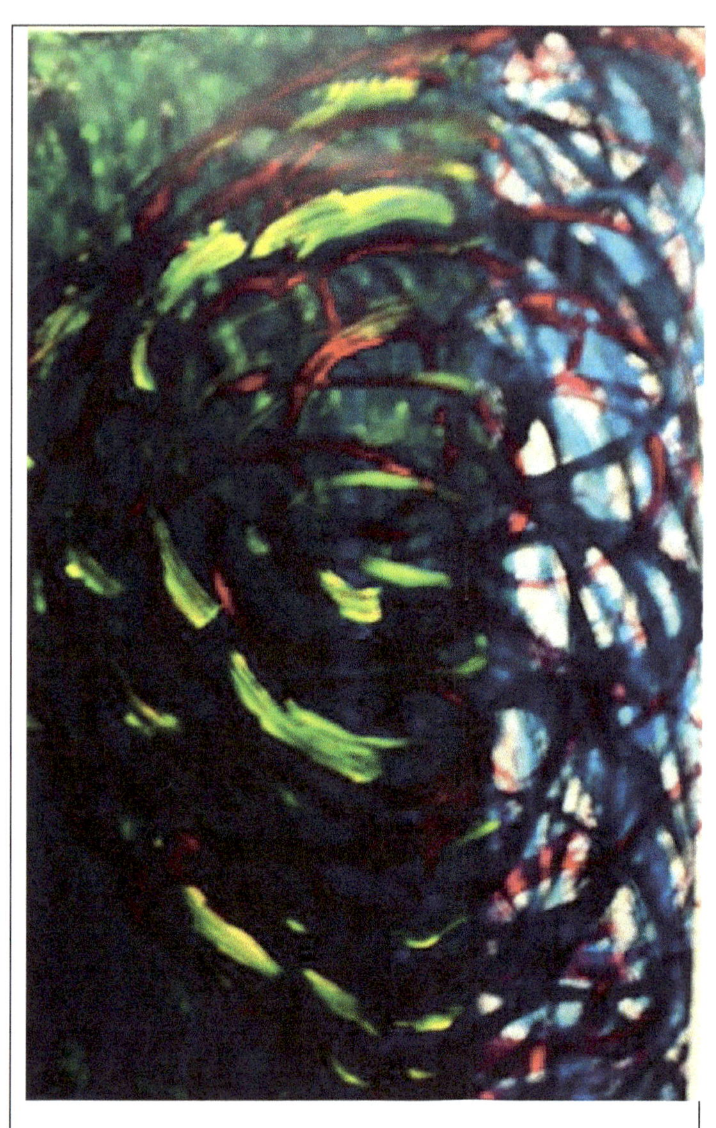

Low as the swerves
Of the sugarbirds
Is love's breathe

And like a fabric torn
There is no future
Save only in burning
Is to see love
In the present ashes

The sound of breaking
Wings, is like
Bones breaking inside
A matchstick heart cracking

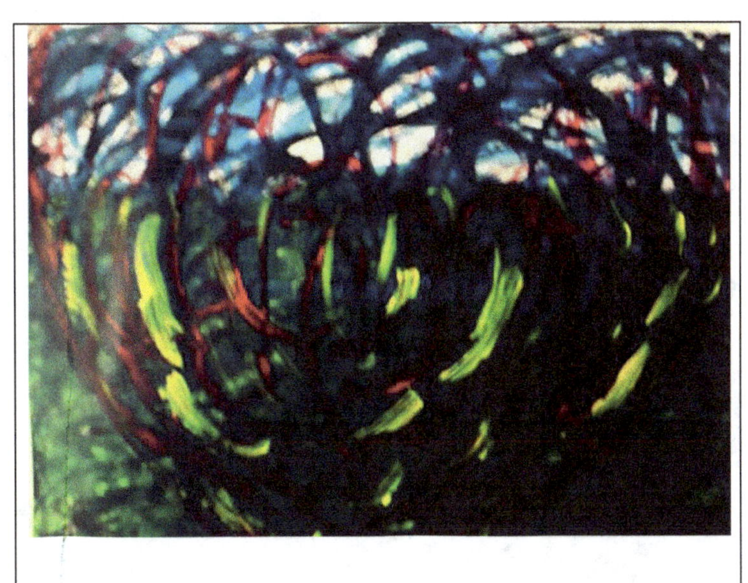

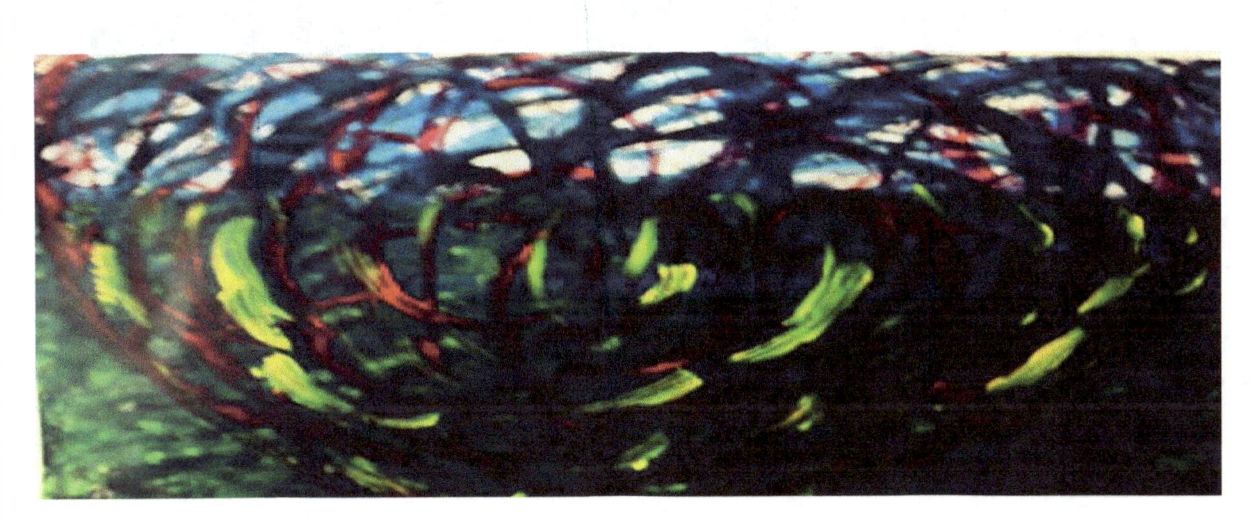

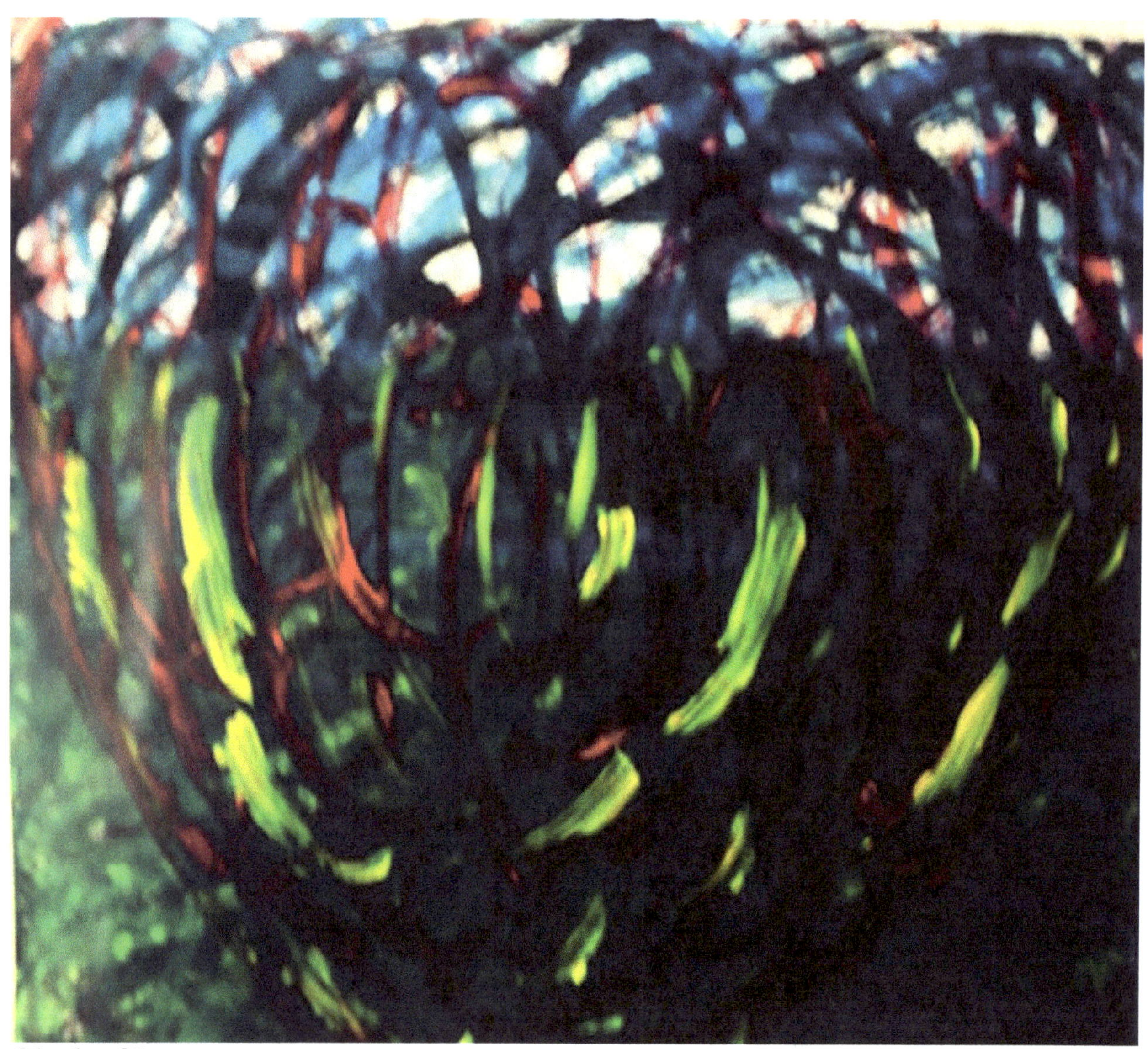

Glyph of Love

JUST BOYS TOGETHER

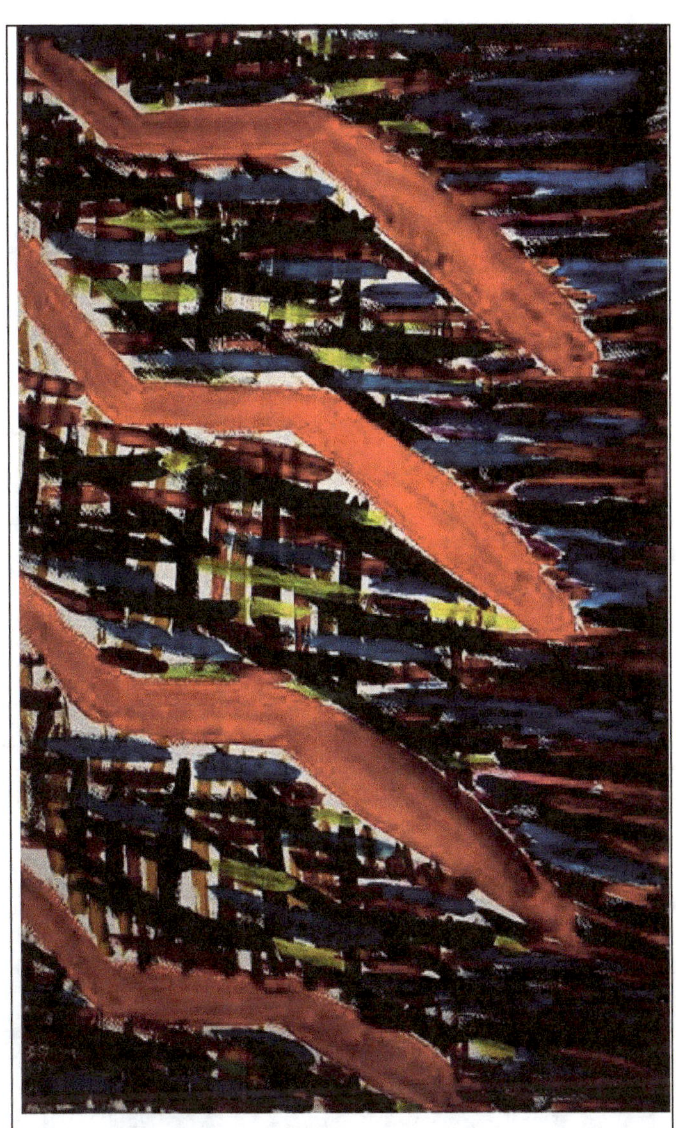

Self-awareness is often unpleasant
I don't find it easier
Distraction is often what I would need

Women to men
Men to women
Like fat sun to bald moon

To continue the species
Is survival behaviour
That changes you

To carry a baby in you
For twelve months like an elephant
Is pain causing behaviour?

Sublimation, deflected energies
Seeking it for yourself
And inflicting it upon others

Is essentially rapist
Not homosexual behaviour

Just boys together
Figures frozen in adolescence
Loyalty to your own pack mate

Is testing behaviour
In the pre-historic park

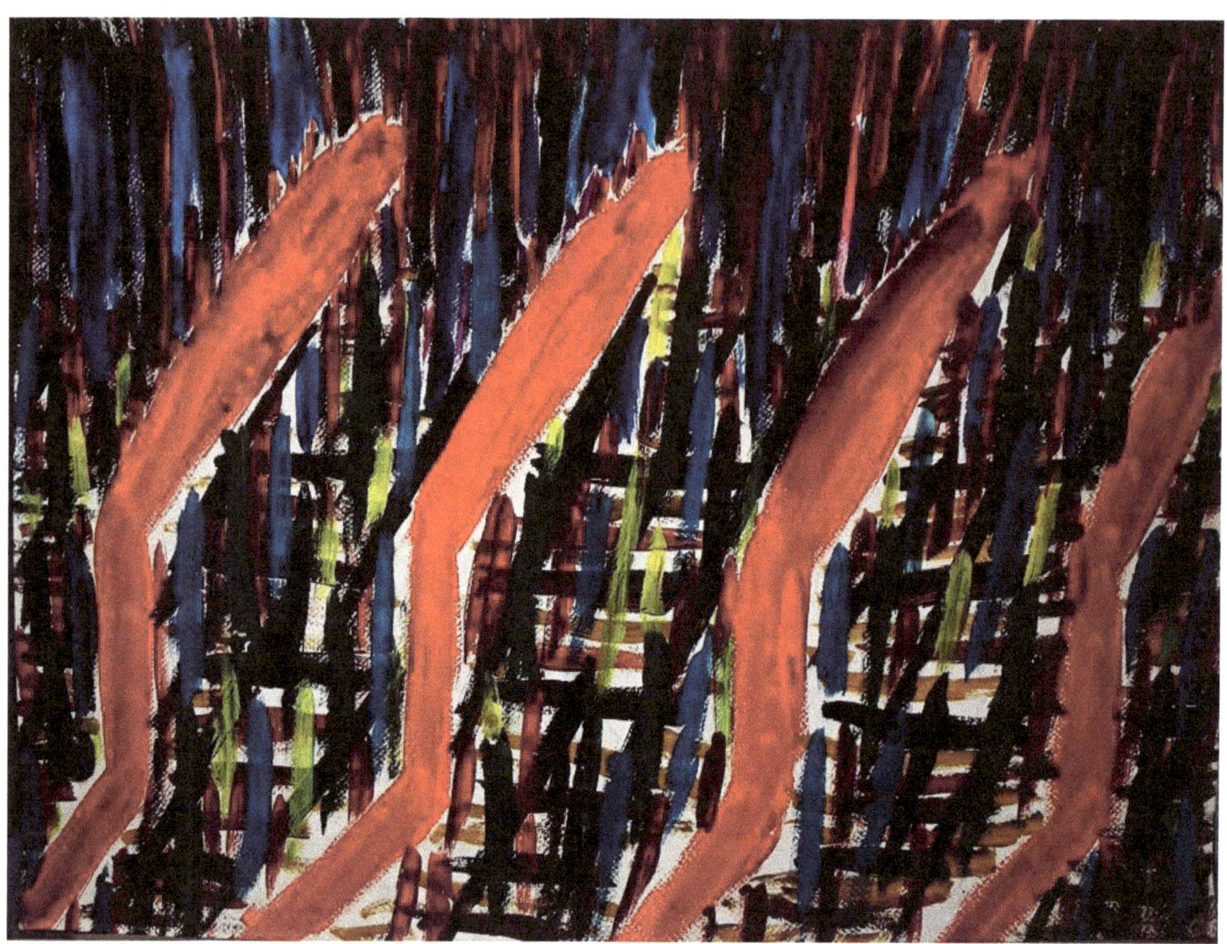

Me and my boys

TELL ME YOU FOOL

What is your life?
When you hold back-
the greatest gift of life.

A pre-space thing of-
old earth.
It is our best hope-
to perpetuate.

But every night a new-
bed and the constant urge,
to run and
displace sex into pain.

You make new babies.
New lives to warp-
and twist.

You don't understand it.
Why does your water-
hates you so much?
And why it is committed to it.

When this water's message
begins to scream.

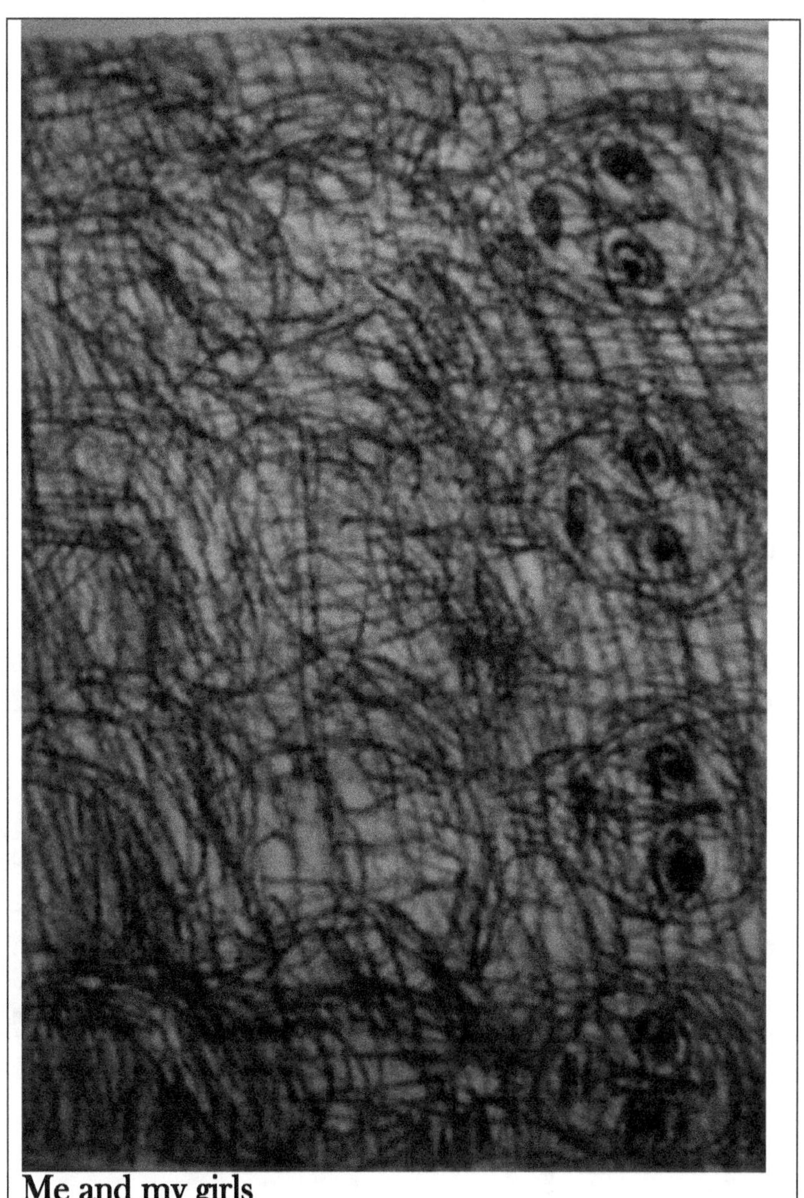

Me and my girls

People start to speak of sex,
not of water in their thirsty.

And they share sex with each-
other and never think,
of parting.

And at night they merge,
move, and hold-
back nothing.

Tell me you fool!
How have you given yourself?
In the face of that.

Tell me you fool!

How have you given yourself?

In the face of that.

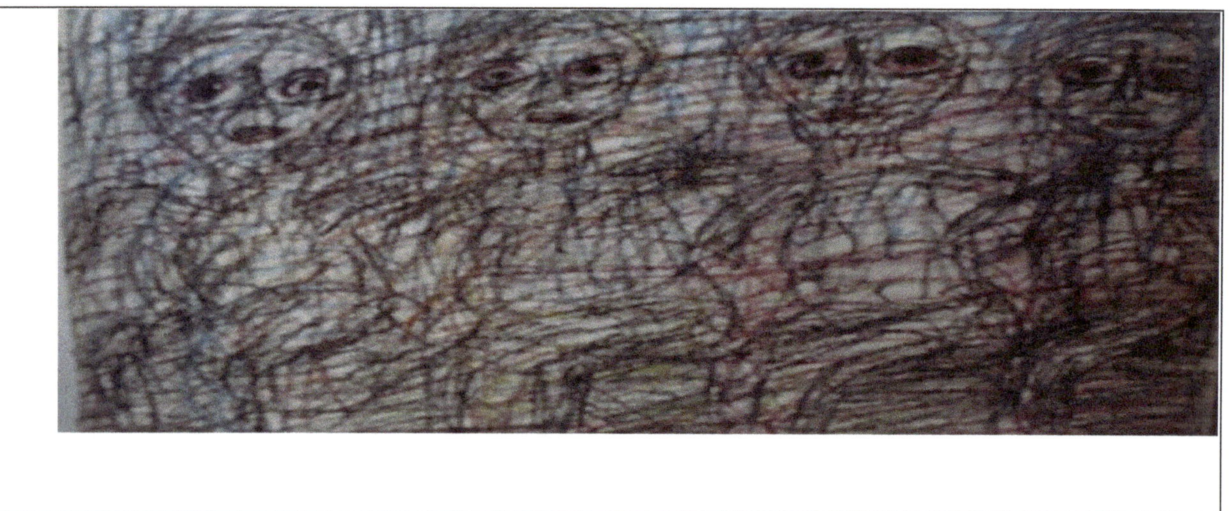

COOKING HER DREAM

she took a pot, filled it with water-
put it on the stove to boil and when-
it was almost boiling she added Maize-meal,
flour, to create a thin porridge and left,
it to simmer, sizzle, and boil.

her Mother, Father, Auntie, and Sister-
were waiting for the food in the dinning room.
making little conversations about-
love, marriage, life, and-
for twenty minutes she snatches-
bits of her family's conversations as,
she keeps an eye on her pot.

after a while she added more-
mealie flour and stir and mixed it.
until she had created Sadza-
a thick, very thick porridge.
and then left it to heat for another-
ten minutes whilst she-
prepared pumpkin-leaves relish.

in a small pot, a little water, she-
added, and a teaspoon of soda.
she lets it boil for a little while and,
then she added cut pumpkin leaves-
tomatoes, onion, salt and cooking oil.

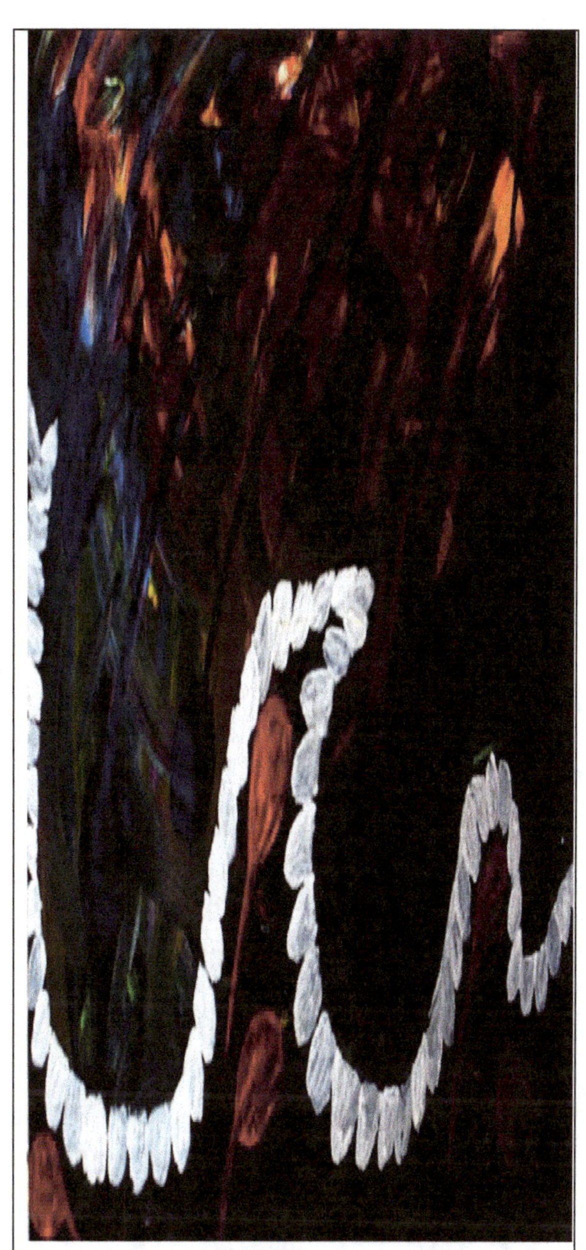

three spoons of peanut-butter and,
then crush, grill, mesh and-
mix this until it had created Mubowora.
an almost porridge, delicious meal,
and she lets it simmer for some minutes.

she serves the Sadza and Mubowora-
to her family, but her family,
says the food has turned bad.
is smelly and decaying and throws it away.
and her own food tastes bad as well-
yet she had just cooked the food.
so she had to cook again!

she cooked the same Sadza again.
and for relish she tried Derere instead.
in a small pot, she added a little water,
and a teaspoon of soda and then,
she lets it boil for a little while.

added cut okra leaves and seed pods,
and a little pumpkin leaves,
onion, tomatoes, salt and cooking oil.
crushed, meshed and mixed it until it had created-
a thin syrup which she served with the Sadza
and this time her family enjoyed the food.
and she also enjoyed it.

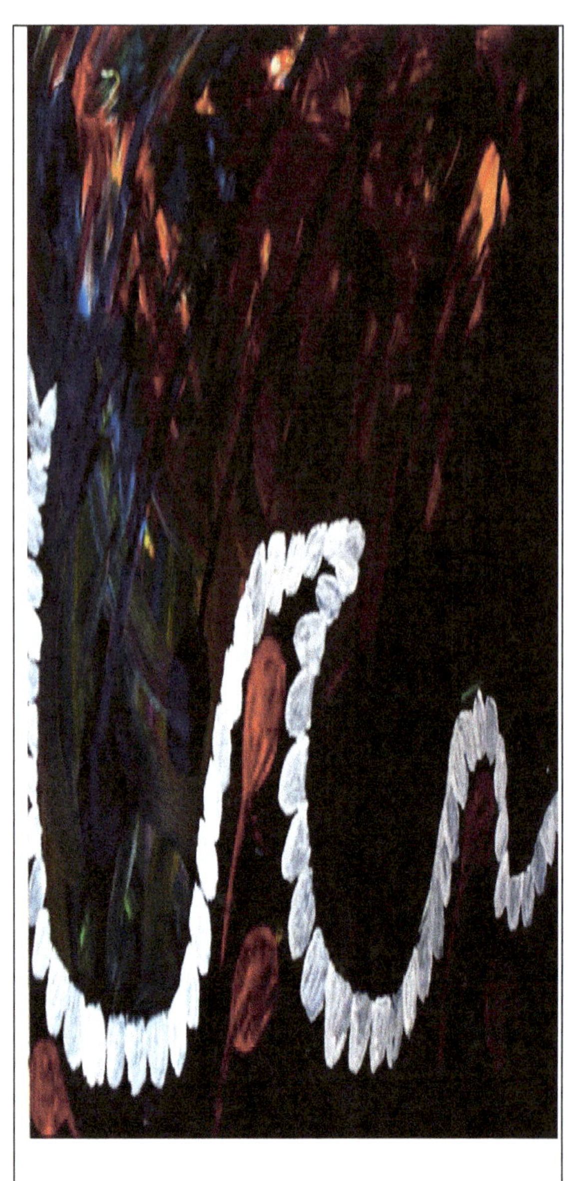

when she told me about this dream-
i had kept counsel and couldn't tell her-
that it meant her current relationship,
with her Chris Brown boyfriend would not last.
and afterwards i couldn't tell her every week,
when she told me that he had beaten-
abused, scolded and raged at her, again and again,
that their relationship was the first meal,
that her family had rejected.

because i have feelings for her and-
since dreams can hang someone up,
like as if they were some Astrologers
with criminal records for their interpretations
i couldn't have told her that i was the second-
meal, she and her family had enjoyed.

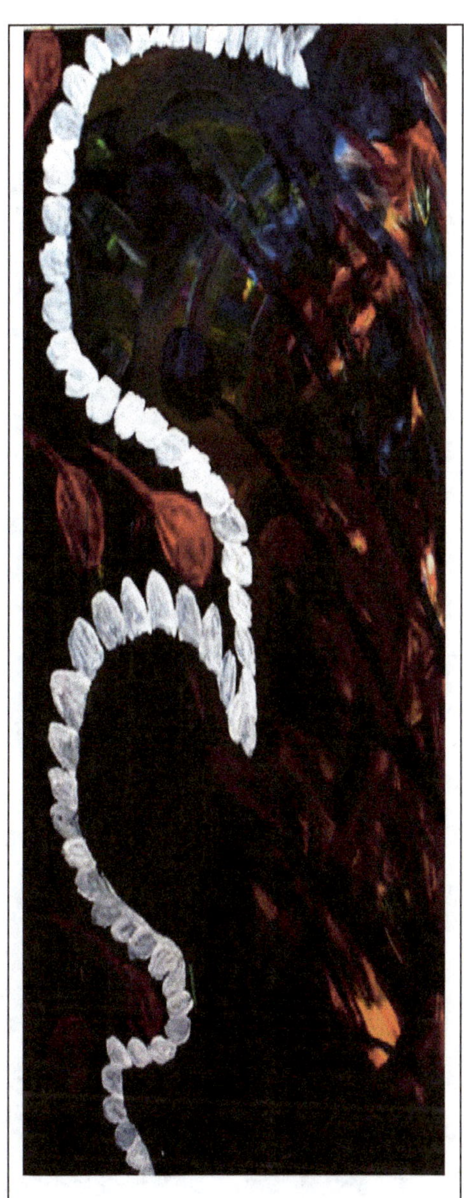

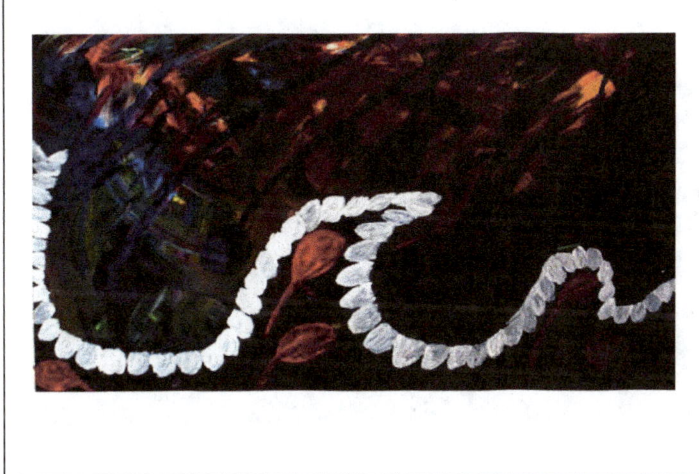

Fertilisation

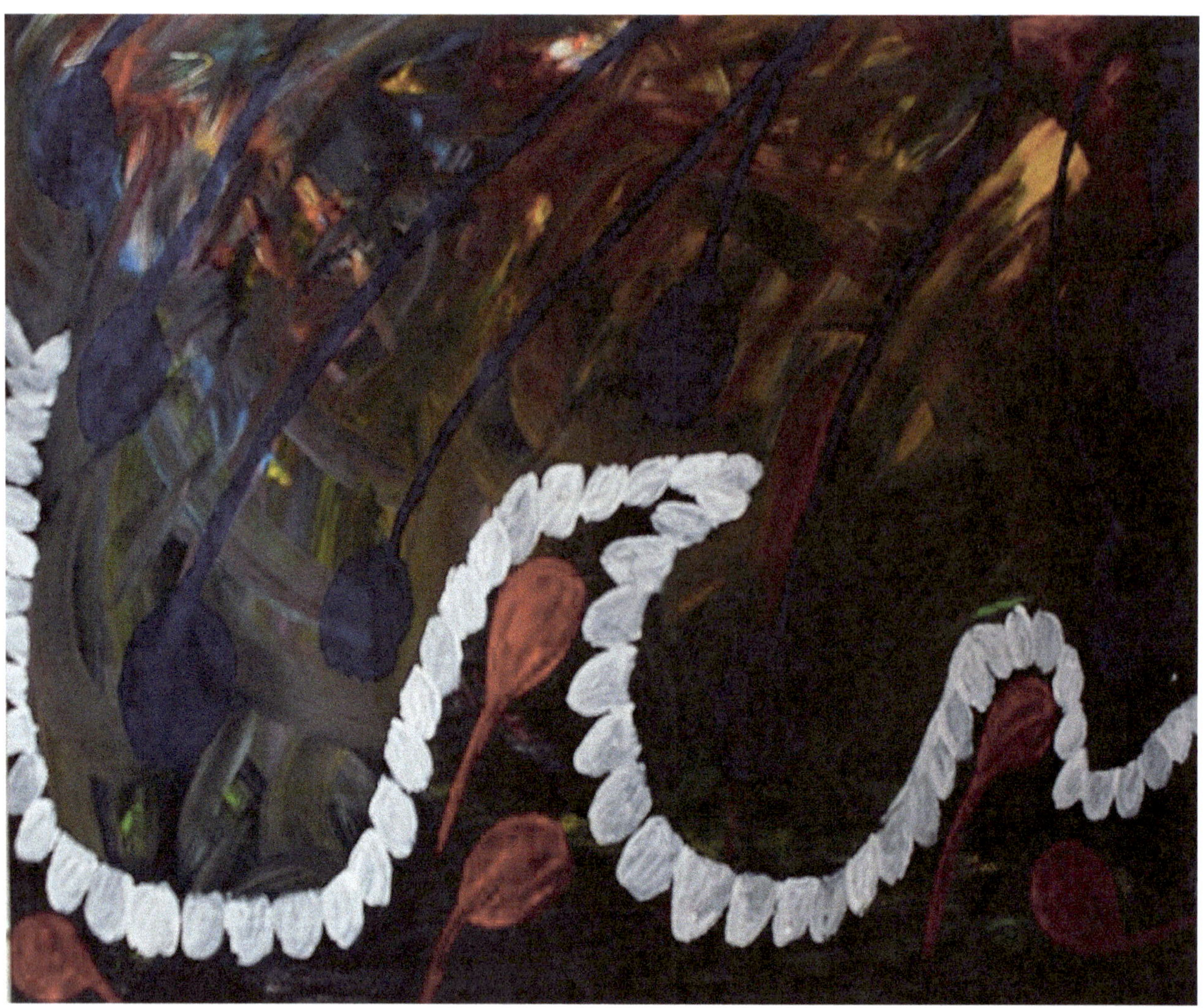

broken connections

She was a woman
A woman of actions
She lived on the front
Filling me with fantasies
Sensations I can't contemplate
Without ecstasies

She was the reasons
She was the justifications
Of my being
Of all that I have ever done

But her laughter drives
Inwards of me
To teach me lessons
Of broken connections

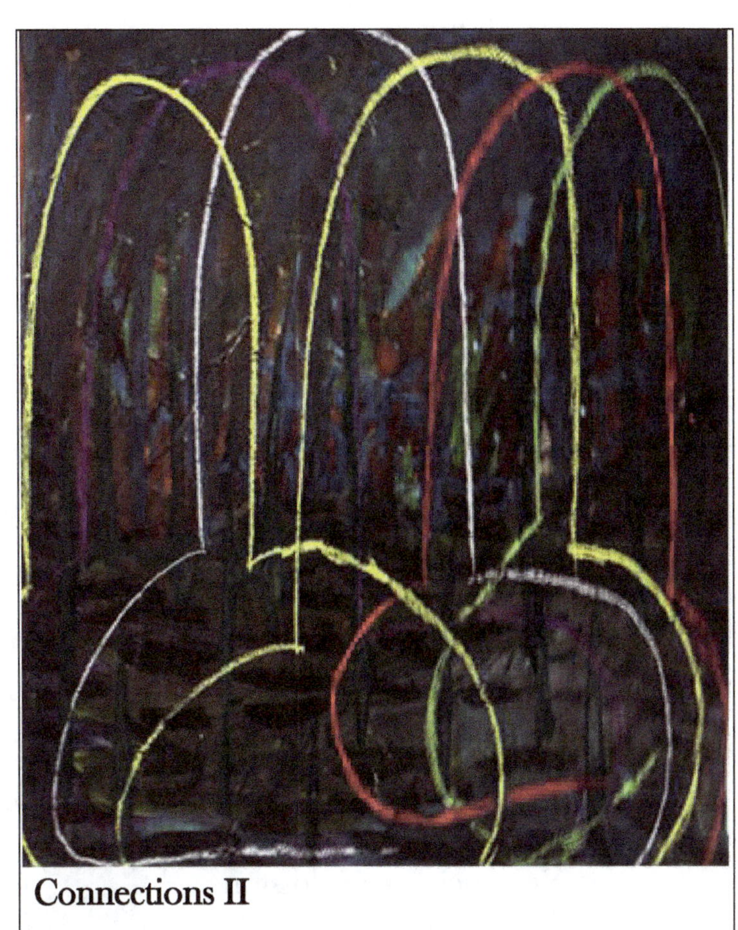

Connections II

A MEMORY LEAF FOR YOU

Always thinking of home
With the sky so blue.
Wafty clouds tucking
The wings of the sky.
We ran through autumn
And rose to meet
Each other's kisses and
March's soft showers.
The winter's colds forcing
Our need of each other.
Stirring the coals of our love-
Our special fare,
Of toasty moments.
Memories wrapped within,
My heart, reminds me-
That my heart is still there.
And of the softness of your voice.
On that sunny golden stone.
That brought me love-
And you that was,
Not stuck on a cold stone.
My mind unwrapping the covers-
Of your youthful flesh.
Thoughts within my flesh,
So warmy, so cosy.

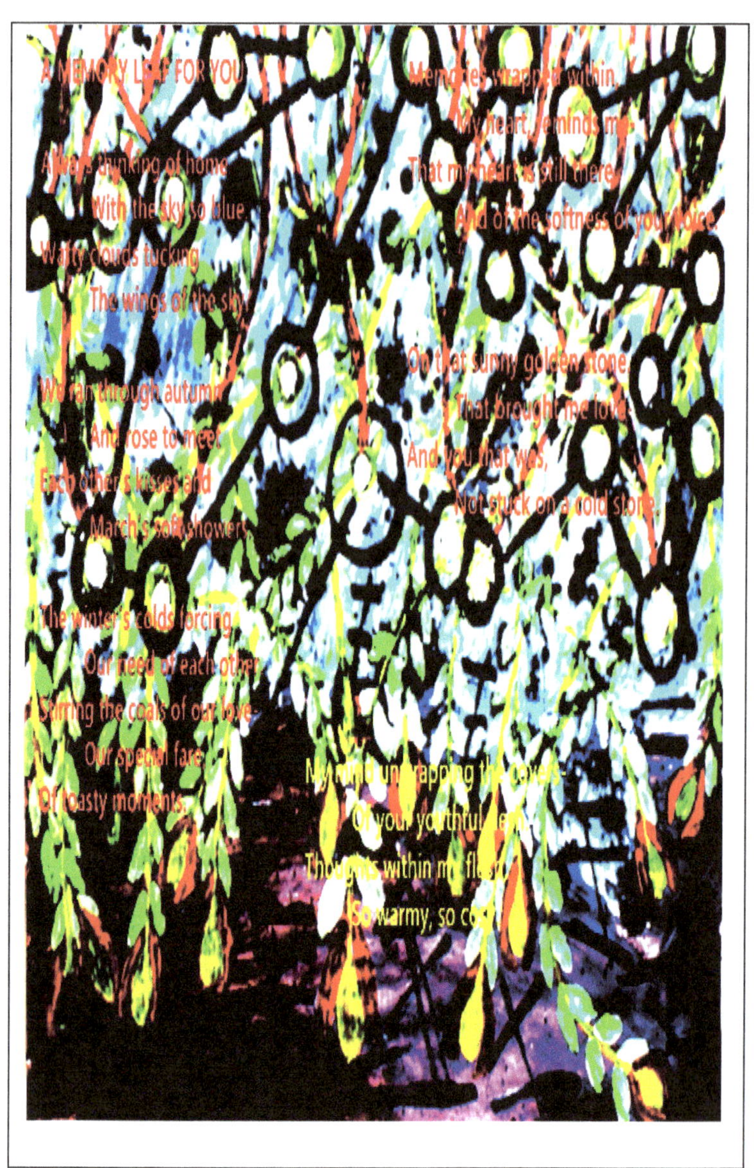

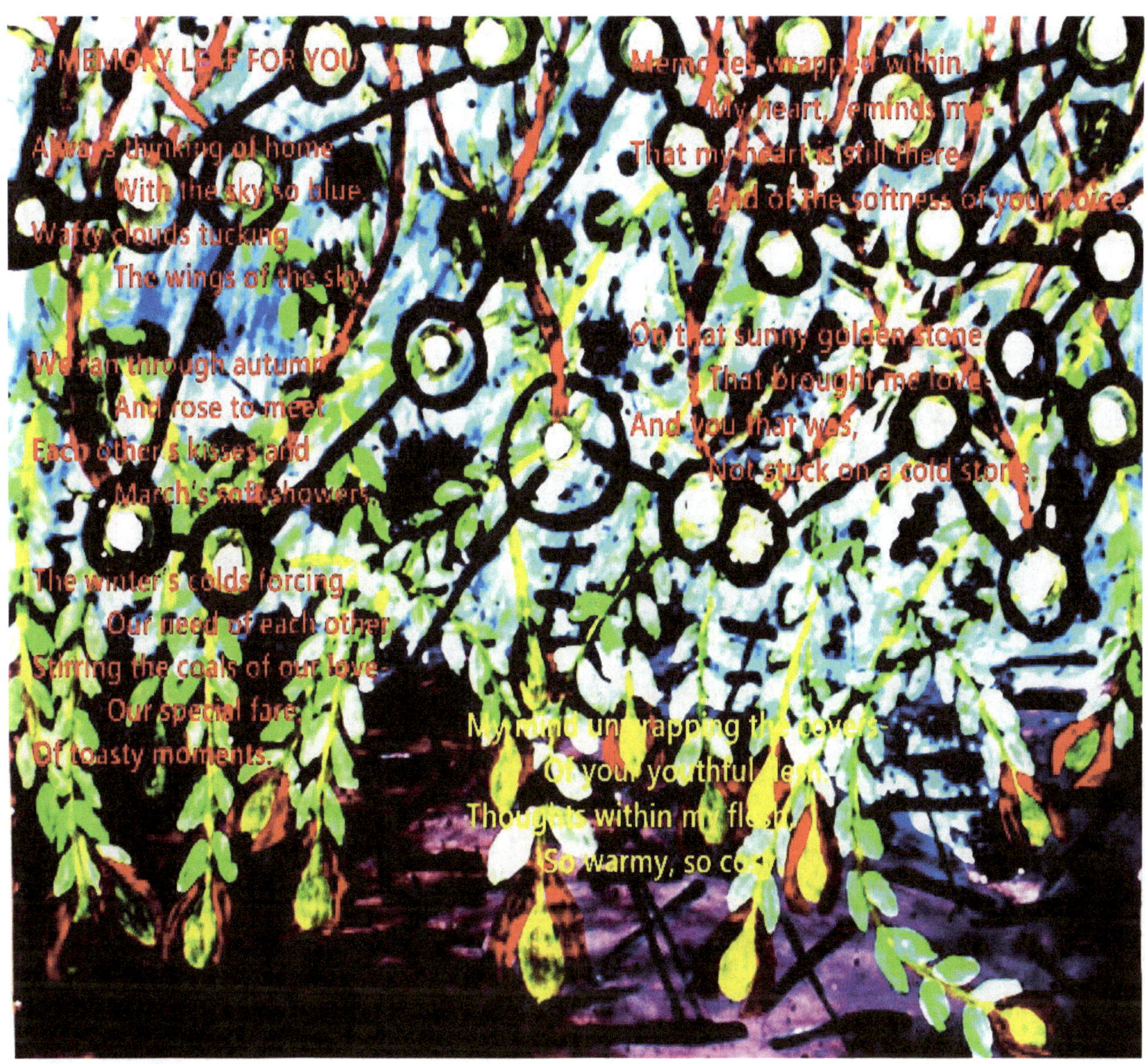

Memory leaves

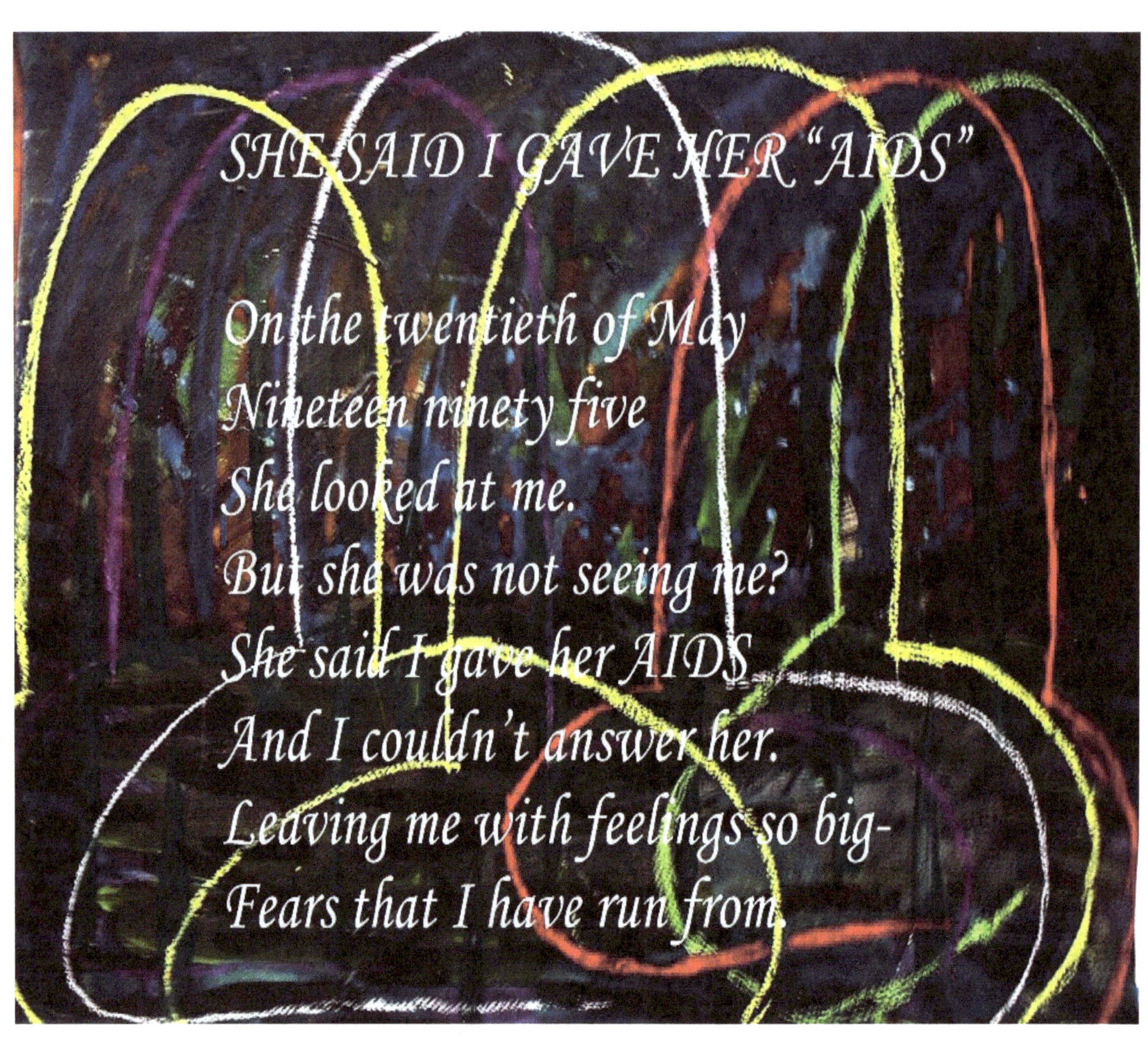
SHE SAID I GAVE HER "AIDS"
On the twentieth of May
Nïneteen ninety five
She looked at me.
But she was not seeing me?
She said I gave her AIDS
And I couldn't answer her.
Leaving me with feelings so big-
Fears that I have run from.

be-longing

after reading Jenna Mervis poem "Shedding Skin."

It has taken you two solid years to think about all this. It has to be the right decision. She deserves it. She's been there for you. Life is swaddled in belonging and ends up swaddled in belonging. One's life in relation to someone's life. A wife's life in relation to husband's life. A girlfriend's life in relation to boyfriend's life. One's death in relation someone's death. Bones in the grave in relation to the soil. Or a person's spirit. Someone's soul in relation to the endower. Or to the devil or even to nothingness. Even life in between is swaddled in belonging. Belonging to someone is the icon of our connections that have galleried all our memories. And shaped us into individuals. Belonging to someone is the mark that has mapped the man-made marriages of our past. Our lives and our futures too.

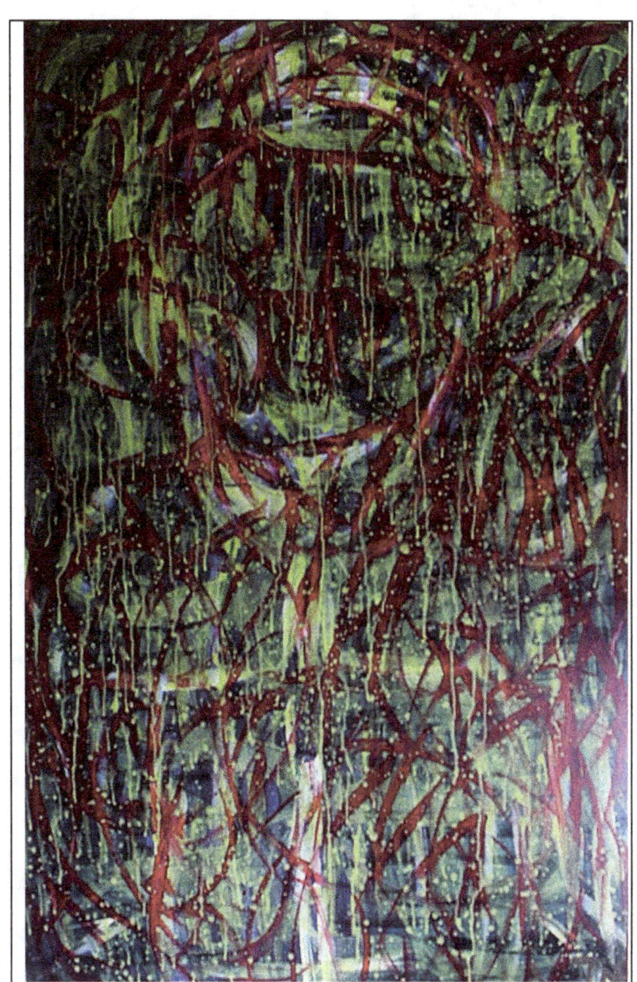

Tears in Heaven

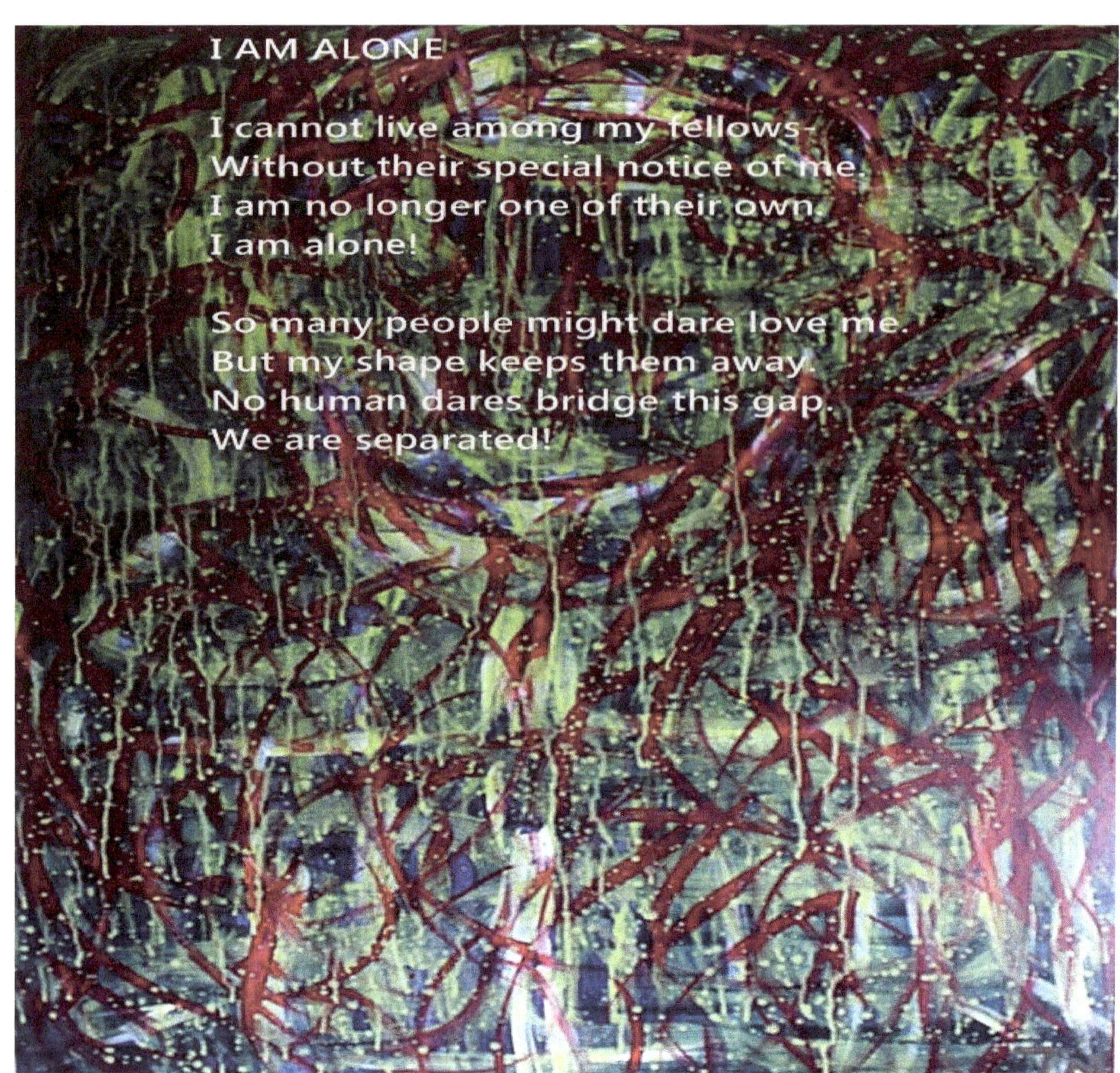
I AM ALONE

I cannot live among my fellows-
Without their special notice of me.
I am no longer one of their own.
I am alone!

So many people might dare love me.
But my shape keeps them away.
No human dares bridge this gap.
We are separated!

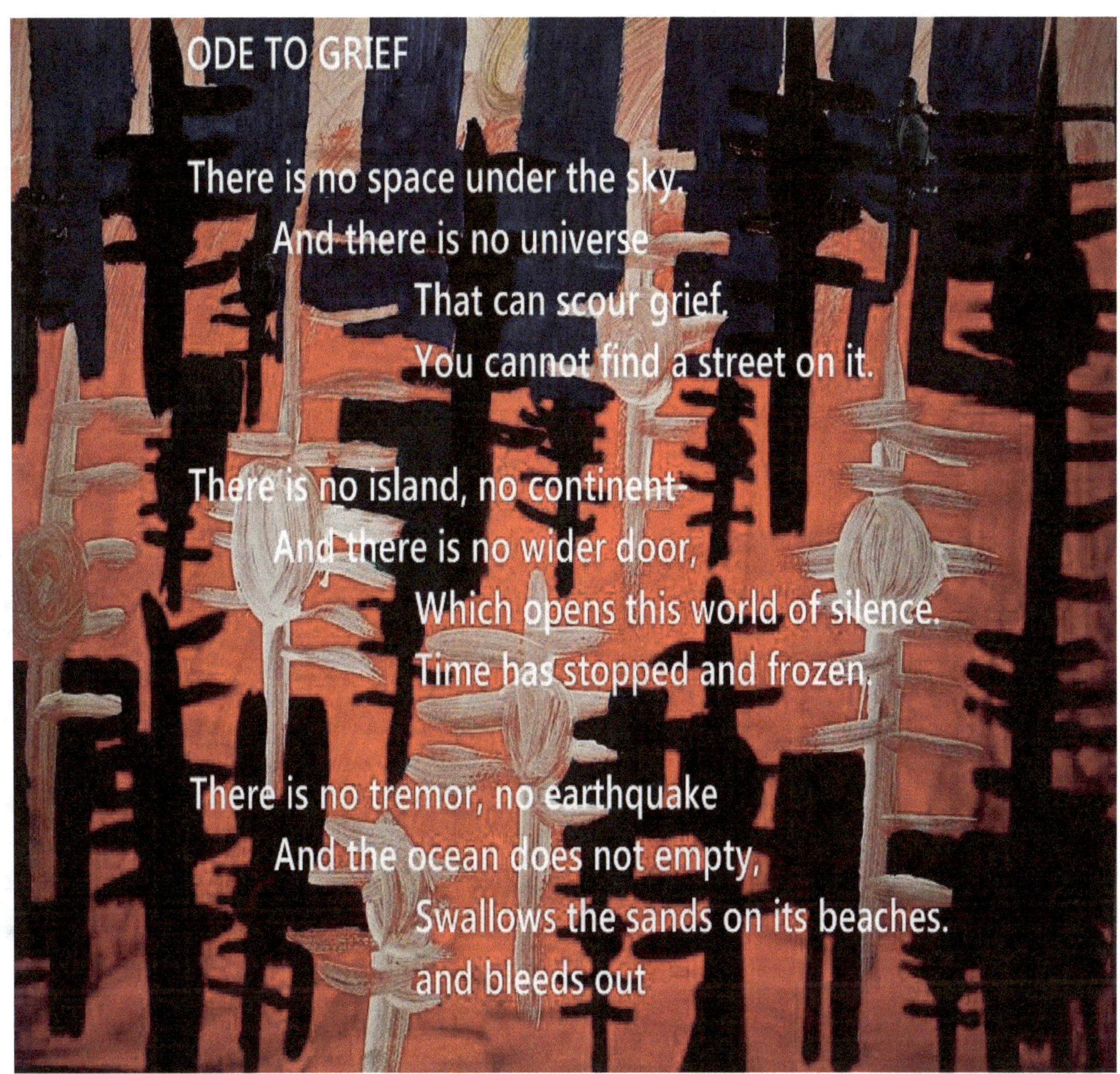

Emblems of archetypes

I CAN PLAY AT BEING UNFEELING

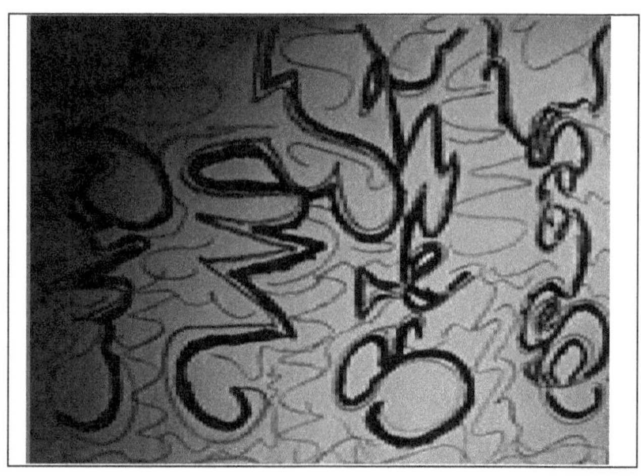

So
many
times I have
fallen in love.

So
many
times I have
watched them go.

Sometimes
they go so quickly.
Sometimes with agonizing slowness.

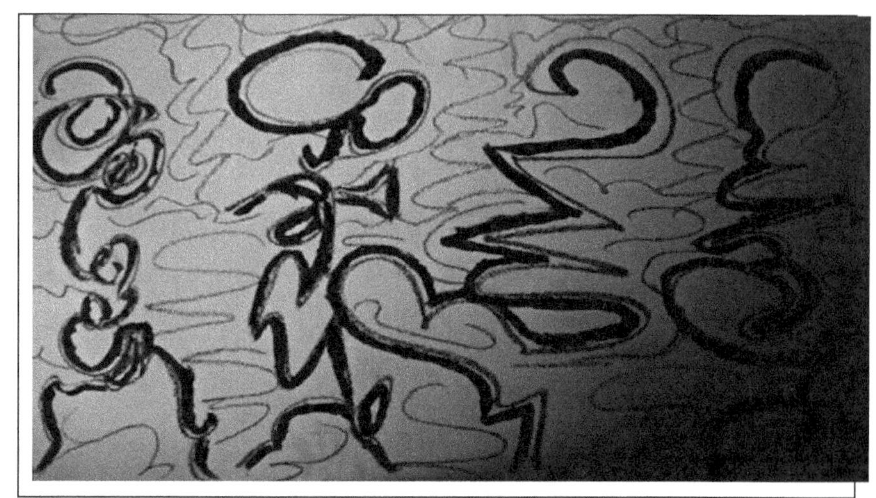

I can
play at being
unfeeling.

I can
make necessary
decisions

But every
time I am wrecked.
For I cannot escape the suffering

And for a
long, long time I live,
In terrible immediacy of emotions.

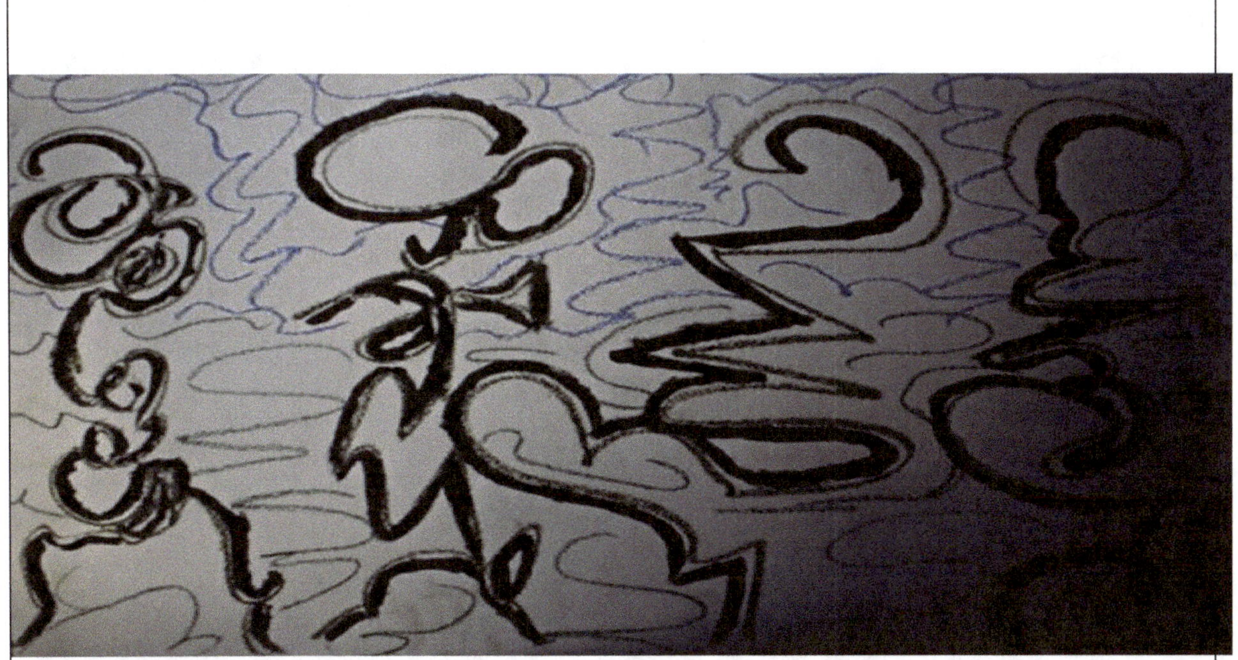

But every
time I am wrecked.
For I cannot escape the suffering

Watching them go

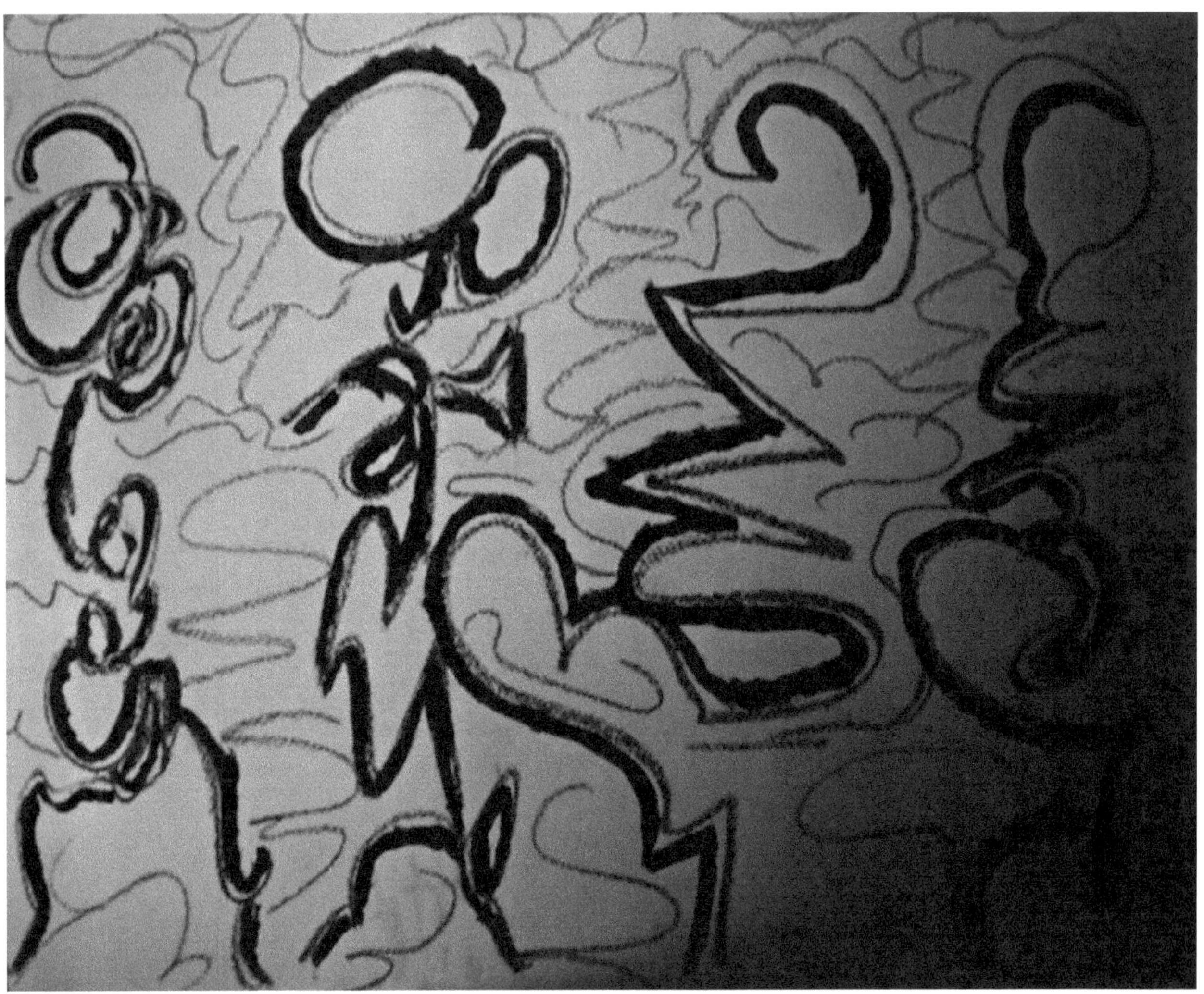

Songs of an alpha male

No women, no love, pleases all alike
Bachelors, love won't kill you, but loving will
For men, nothing is certain but bachelorhood
For a woman, it is love and marriage.

Everyone can find love, few can do better
Finding happiness!
Happiness takes no account of love.

Love make houses, marriage makes homes
Marriage is the touch and tone of a brave love
Love is a treasure, but sex is the key!

I have isolated the love-sex experience
A lot of women use sex to control their men
But love-makers often burn their fingers
For sex can be so lethal.

Love is the mother of marriage
Love is easy, dating and marriages are harder
They create pressures that often erupts
But love well and you are two-thirds marriage

Love rules the woman, marriage rules the man

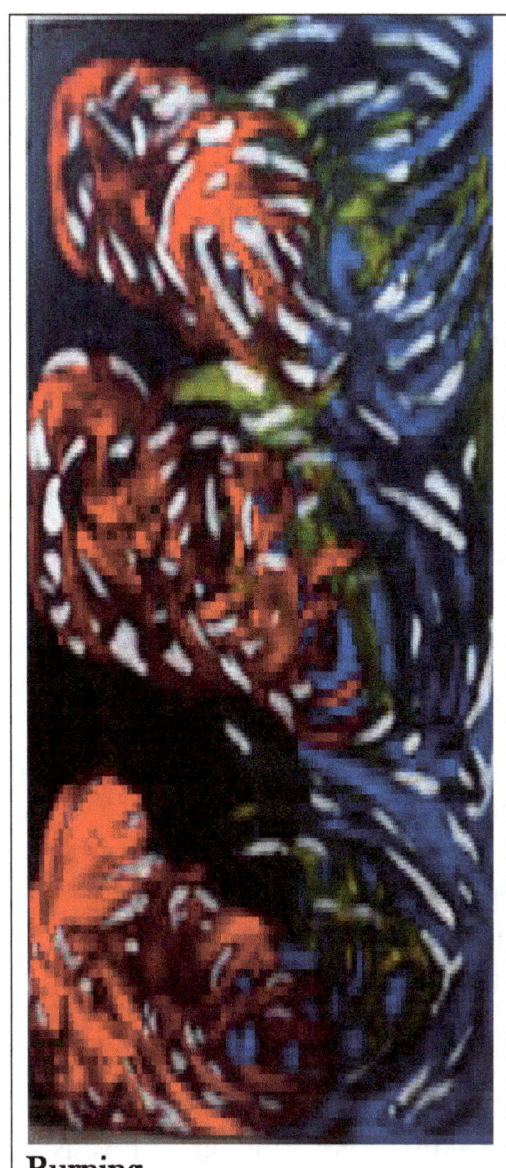

Burning

Love makes a man fit for any work
For money does more, but love much more

Nature's first law is love
Nature never meant us for love and marriage
So love another's wife but don't put yours away

No and no are the only causes to all love's disputes
And when a woman is not loved
Whatever she does, whoever she is, is always amiss

He who wants love cannot find an easy chair
Love without understanding is
A violet without smell

Love without a return is
A question without an answer
Too much of love is good for nothing
So love not to live but live to love

Good love brings shame, bad love joy
My son put not your trust in love
But put you love into trust

Love burdens, long borne, grows heavy
And love is half-spent before we know what it is
For little love is loud, great love is silent

Love leads the willing, but drives the stubborn

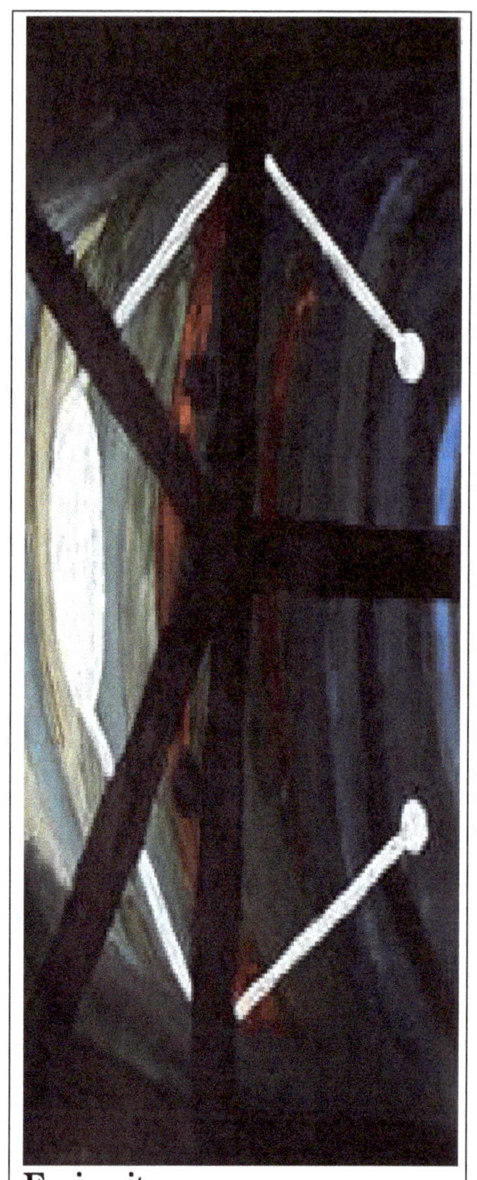

Facing it

Love only when you can afford to lose
Kindle not a love that you cannot put out.

Love is a fire, it wants both feeding and watching
Love, when it is too hot, it is too dangerous
Love is like a fire, once out, it is hard to rekindle

The newer the love, the sweeter the tune
So love well when you are loved well
Good love always makes good love

For it is love alone
That makes us always willing to live
So choose your love and love your choice

Love reaches further than long arms
Loving well is a woman's best revenge
Her love is so sweet, but she stings!

Nearest to the heart, nearest to heartbreak
Love is the greatest lie this world has ever seen
The world would perish were all men in love

Love is a remedy for everything
Could men find it?
There is too much love that loving

Love is not what it is
But what it seems

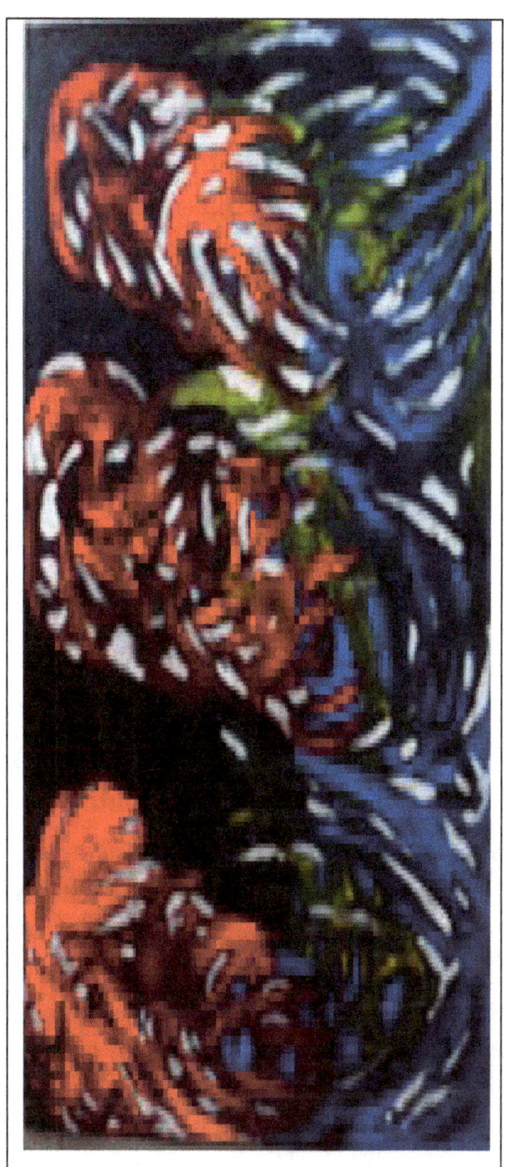

Seeming and seeming
Like the balls in a juggler's hands

Nothing is love, nothing is true
And nothing really matters
For nothing that is love is permanent

When love is asleep, and if I were you
I would not wake it up
But better you love than I love

When only one is in love, the other one is happy
When both are in love, both are in the wrong
One half of love does not know how the other loves

No love is ill if she be silent
But love and never fear son
Because love makes us foolish, and more wiser
You can see why love is always so dangerous

He who has no love, need no heart
None as deaf as those that love not
None as blind as those that love not
Love shared is made lighter

Absence sharpens love, presence destroys it
Nothing sharpens love like infatuation
Lover's hearts are tied in cobwebs

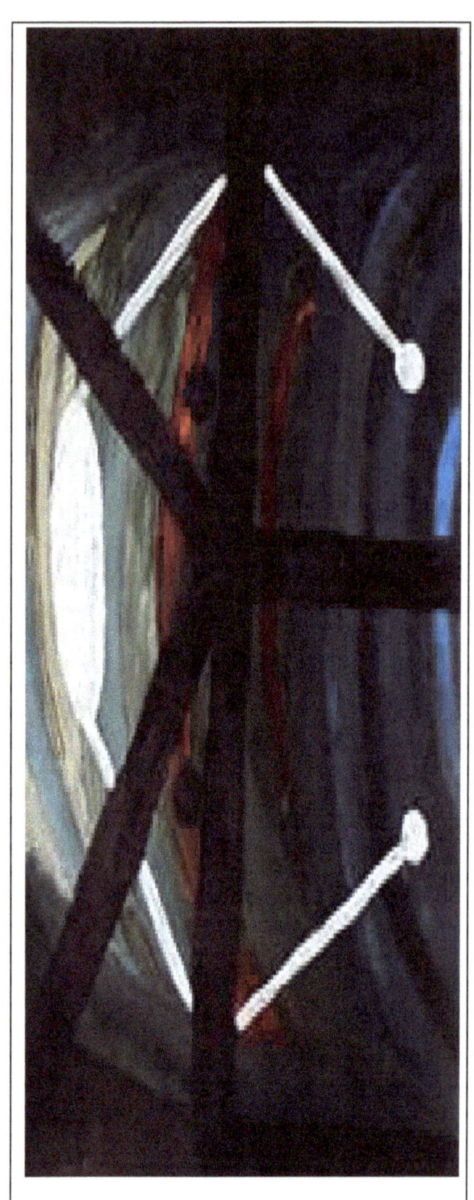

Man proposes, woman disposes
Love is a good servant, but a bad master
Love cannot persuade where it cannot punish

Where no love is, there needs no pardon
Love like lent, love to repent
Love at a haste, but repent at leisure
He loves best who loves last.

Firmness asks for faith
And faith asks for love
Never love someone with love until love loves
For love borrowed is soon sorrowed

Love is the picture of the mind
Throw your love away when you see the new moon
Love comes on wings but depart on foot

Love is for those who want to believe in it
Love is often abused not refused
Love is never good until lost.

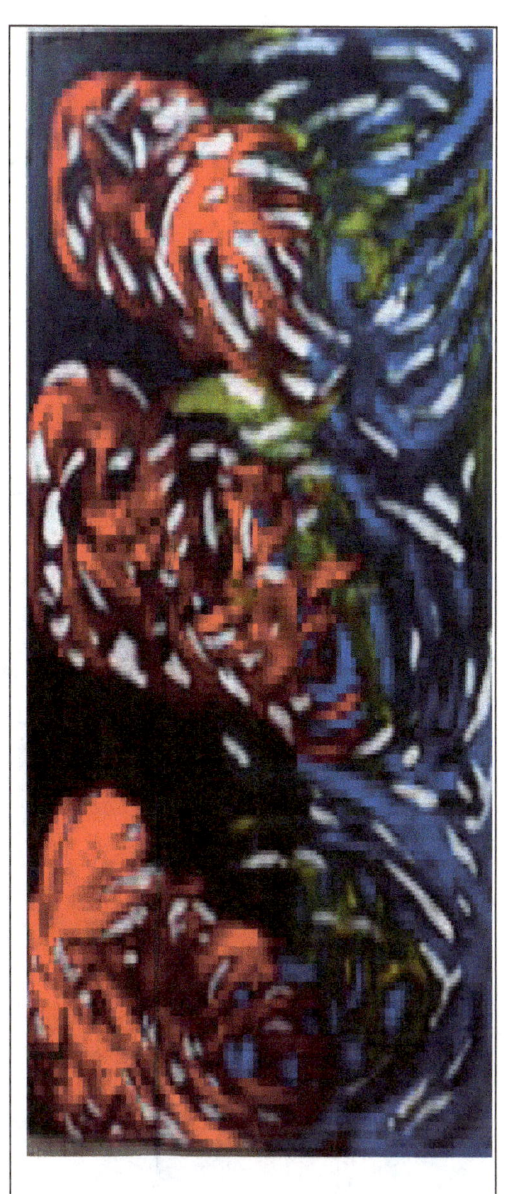

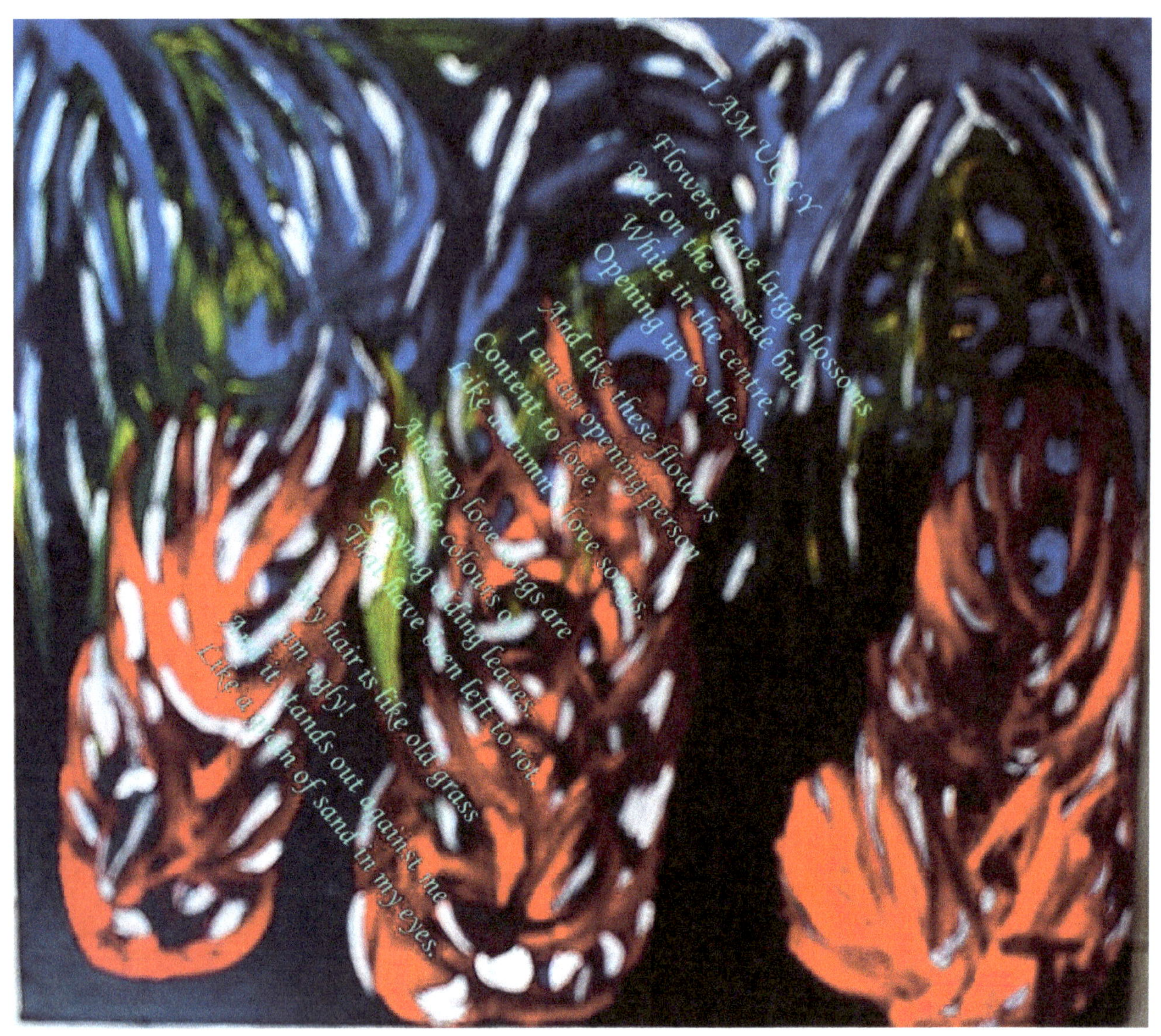
I AM UGLY
Flowers have large blossoms
Red on the outside but
White in the centre.
Opening up to the sun.
And like these flowers
I am an opening person
Content to love.
Like autumn's love songs.
And my love songs are
Like the colours of
fading leaves.
That have been left to rot.
My hair is like old grass
I am ugly!
And it stands out against me
Like a grain of sand in my eyes.

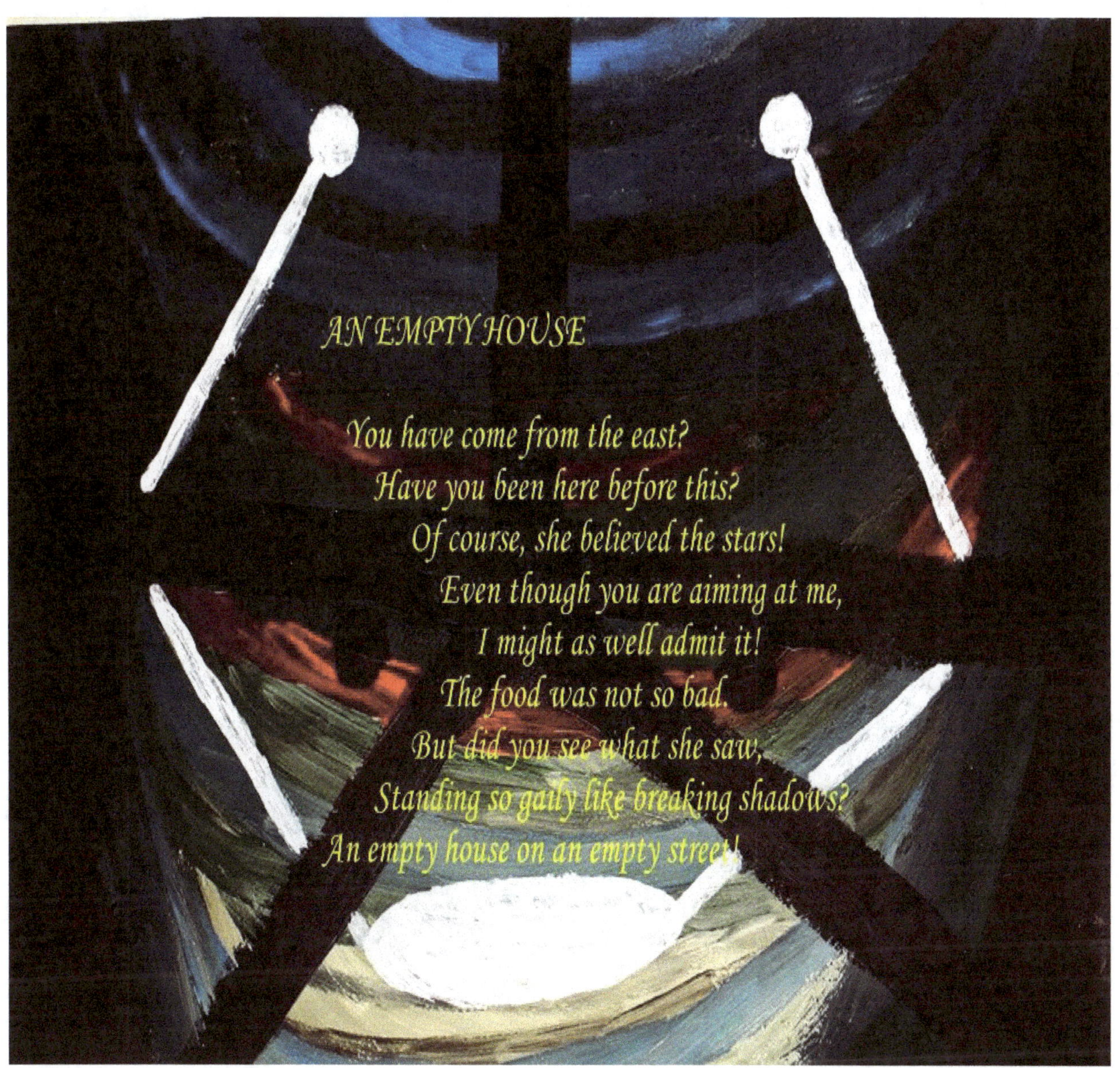
AN EMPTY HOUSE
You have come from the east?
Have you been here before this?
Of course, she believed the stars!
Even though you are aiming at me,
I might as well admit it!
The food was not so bad.
But did you see what she saw,
Standing so gaily like breaking shadows?
An empty house on an empty street!

after reading Arja Salafranca's poem "snake."

You are trying to picture a tapeworm. Burrowing into your skin. You are seeing it with your own eyes. Entering you through your legs. You also know that there is nothing that you can do about it. Most of it already is inside your legs. So you let it enter believing that it would never survive your inside environment. But afterwards you start to feel its suck, suck. Sucking the blood and juices of your legs! Think; just think of its suck, suck, sound and feeling. Sometimes it brings out mucus. Sometimes clotted blood and sometimes smelly sickly waters. Think of it as if it has been in your body for years and years. See yourself ballooning rather than thinning out. One day it stops this sucking. Becomes dormant in your legs. Nestled in the warm insides of your legs. Waiting for another suck, suck time. Then some day out into the future you discover that it hadn't really been dormant. That it had been silently chewing your insides. That all that is now in your insides is just a hollow space. The library of your gut is now an empty parking lot. Like a life coming to itself!

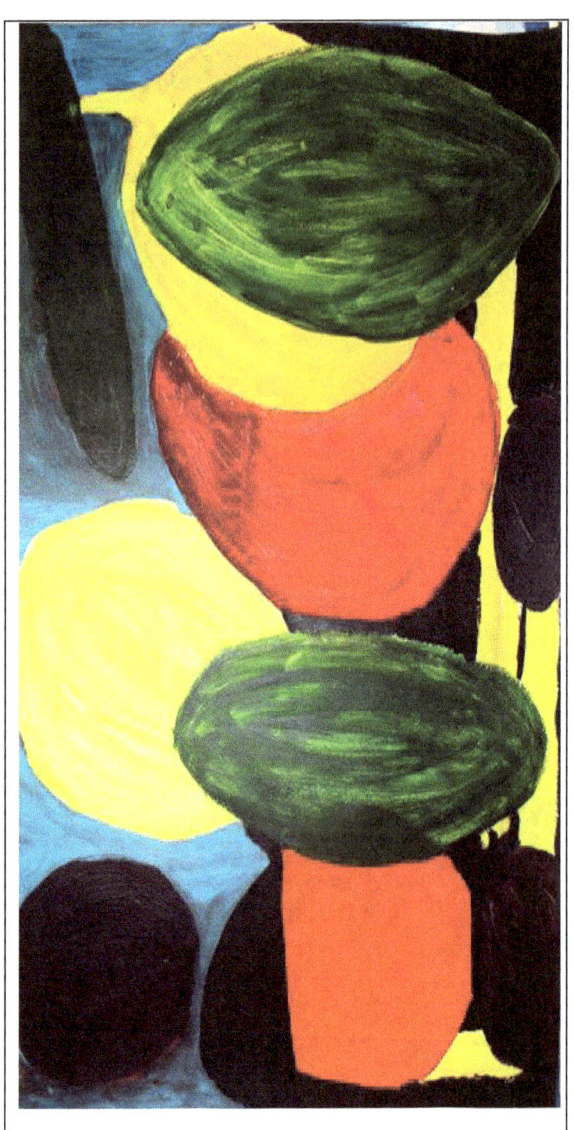

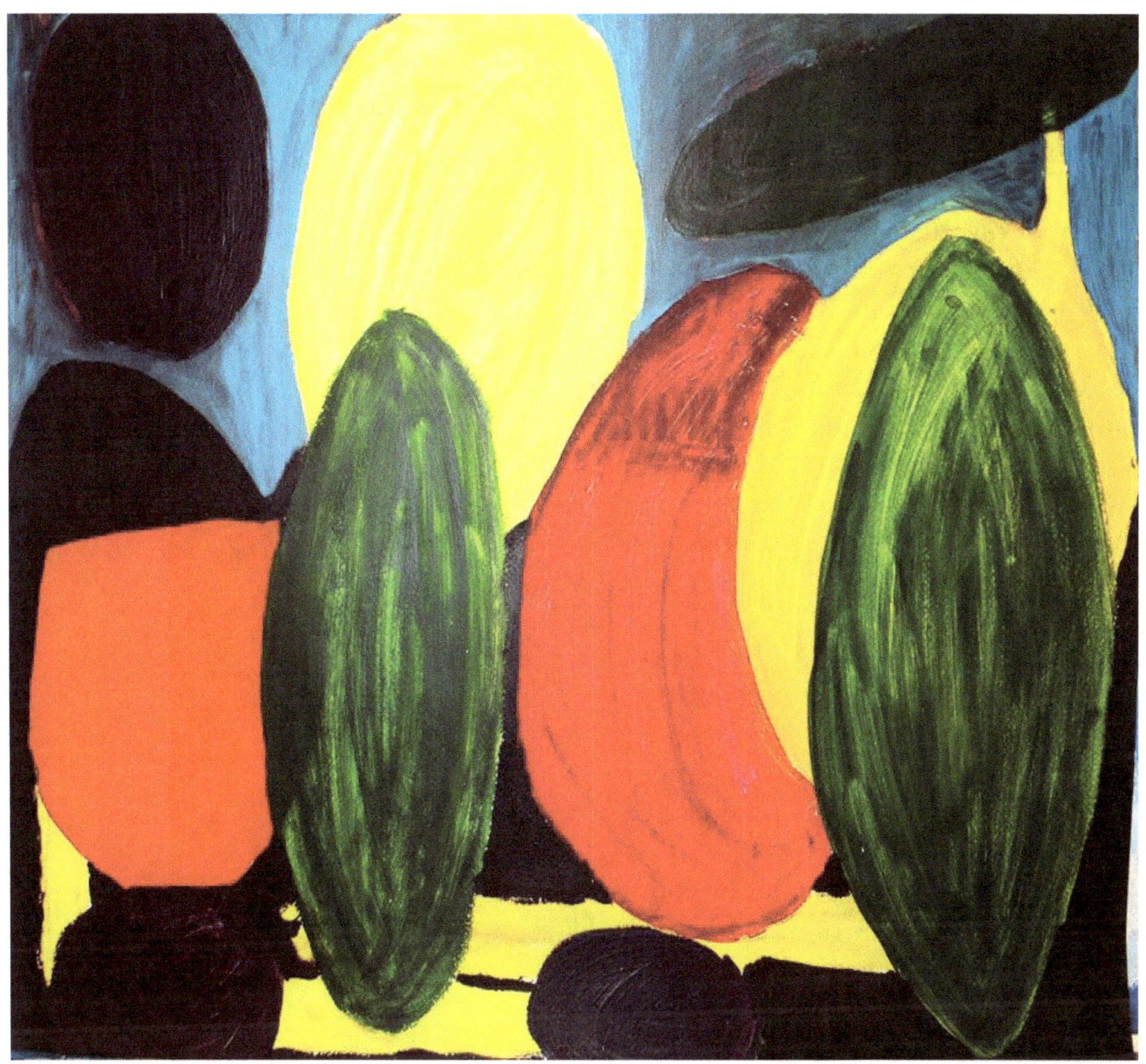

Fruits

WHAT'S SHE LIKE?

What's she like when you tell her that you love her
and you hold her in your arms, what's she like?
What's she like when she says she loves you?
Is she the constructs of your dreams?
The river that river your life?
What's she like to you?

What she like when you are making love to her
and when she says goodnight tonight, what's she like?
What she like when she wakes by your sides?
Is she the red petals of your heart?
Your love story unfolding in your heart?
What's she like to you?

What's she like when you gaze into her eyes
and she smiles at you, what's she like?
What's she like when you have found your answers?
Is she the tent of your heart's lyricisms?
Wing beats like those of the wingspan?
What's she like to you?
What's she like when she walks by your side
And her hair turns grey on you, what's she like?
What's she like, she that you have chosen?
Is she still busy collecting all the garbage?
That you have dumped on your heart
What's she like to you?

What's she like when she says she is leaving you
and you are begging her to stay, what's she like?
What's she like when she says no more to you?
Is she like blue air flowing out-outer?
And in-inner through the windows?
What's she like to you?

What's she like when she is gone away
And you are crazy about her, what's she like?
What's she like when years have worn hard?
Is she still spinning diamond threads?
And pepper threads of longing?
What's she like to you?

What's she like when memories of her have faded
And you are trying too harder to remember, what's she like?
What's she like when you don't remember her anymore?
Is she a life size dream of your dreaming?
Your dying, your winter?
What's she like to you?

I WILL WARM YOU

Everything has a flame
Within it.
Some flames are dull.
Some are very bright.

My flame burns inside me.
My flame never dies-
And I am never cold.

I am always warmer
Like a hammock.
And if you will curl closer-
I will warm you.

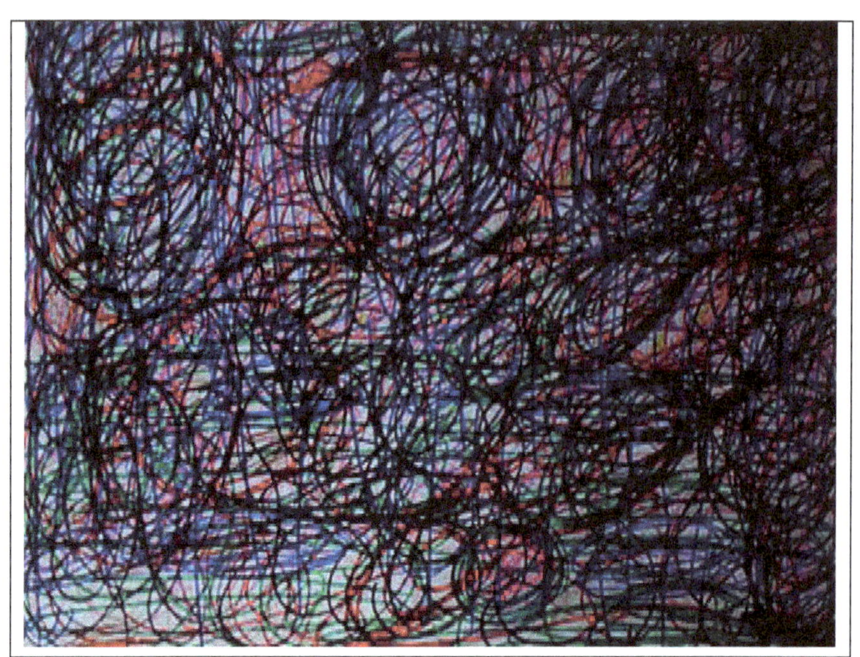

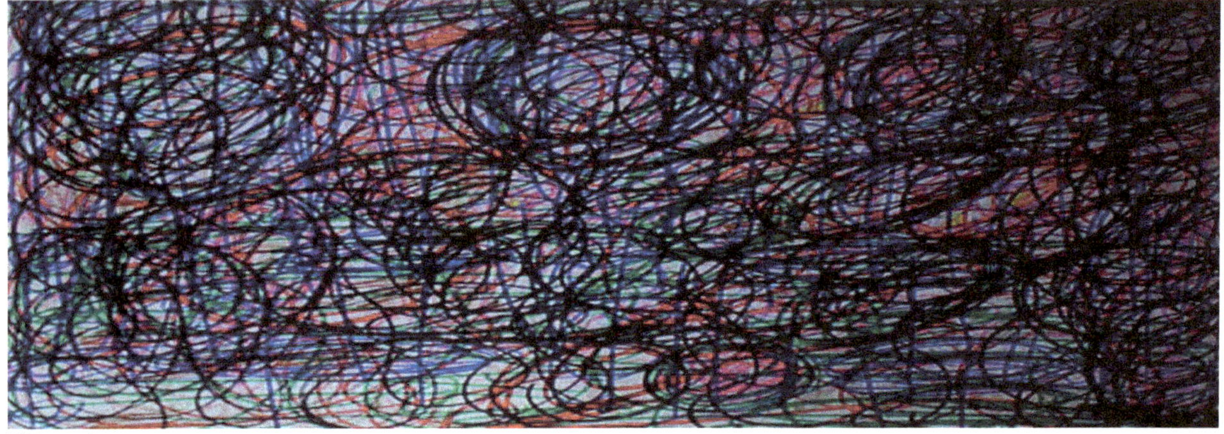

Hugging

I AM THE DESERT

Everything is flat,
A barren massive void of great emptiness.
Everything is quite,
An ocean's full of silent faceless grains.

I am the desert!
I am giving you this opportunity to enter.
I am the desert!
You can take a good look at me.

Blast of sandstorms!
The mad swirling eternal winds; the dust devils!
A blanket of sand,
And this sand might slid down and bury you.

I am the desert!
Darkness befell over me like a curtain.
I am the desert!
I can sense turmoil beneath your wary feelings.

An eerie roll!
Vast salt lakes, mountain dunes, granite hills.
Is that all?
The harsh breeze, the freezing heat- inhospitable!

I am the desert!
I feast away assuming strengths and attitudes.

I am the desert!
Sometimes someone wanders in and get lost.

Remnant animals!
The plants, vultures and night creatures.
And what else?
Behind every questioning belies doubting.

I am the desert!
Some few people are still venturing inside.
I am the desert!
Everything changes and it sometimes rains.

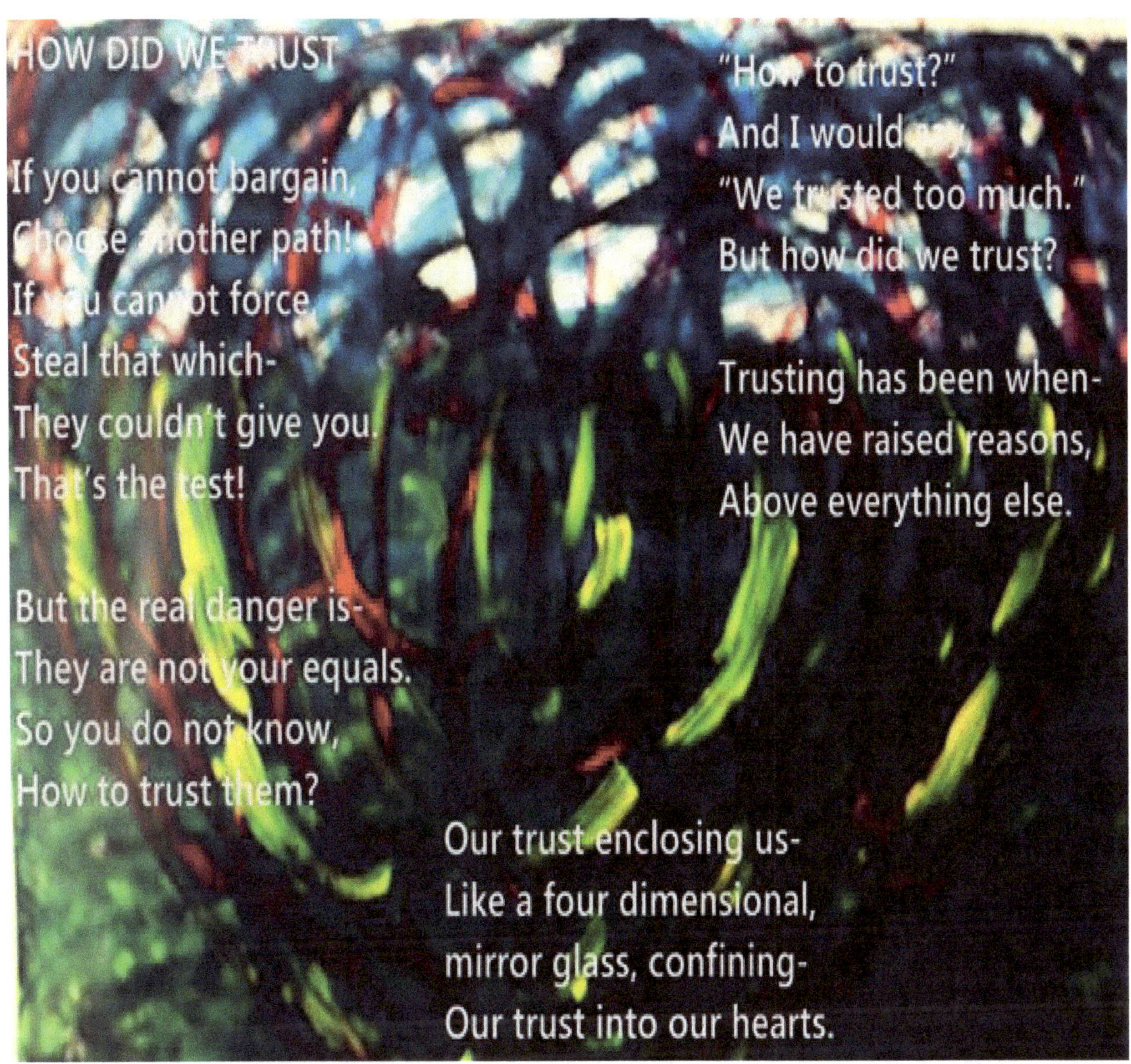

HOW DID WE TRUST

If you cannot bargain,
Choose another path!
If you cannot force,
Steal that which-
They couldn't give you.
That's the test!

But the real danger is-
They are not your equals.
So you do not know,
How to trust them?

"How to trust?"
And I would say,
"We trusted too much."
But how did we trust?

Trusting has been when-
We have raised reasons,
Above everything else.

Our trust enclosing us-
Like a four dimensional,
mirror glass, confining-
Our trust into our hearts.

the language of love

Engaged by the resonances of the language of love. Relying on the tricks of your mind getting you home. You have bought into this marriage thing. For the two years you have been seeing the other. Your mind has spread out; away from you. Has no more plain symbols. Charts or helpful indexes. The last summer lumbered to its inevitable end. The way a song modulates from minor to major chords. Achieving dissonance, consonance, and harmony. Then dies in the listener's ears. She like the previous summer has already left, without your noticing it. She has no more plans for you this winter. But you have continued to believe in your love for her. Even when her perfume has wafted into the thin blue air. And the magic has died down? Unless you know the quality of your soil: these seeds of your errors can creep upon the path of your feelings. Your small stories already wondering away. And the only story could be the one that lies ahead, of all these small stories of yours.

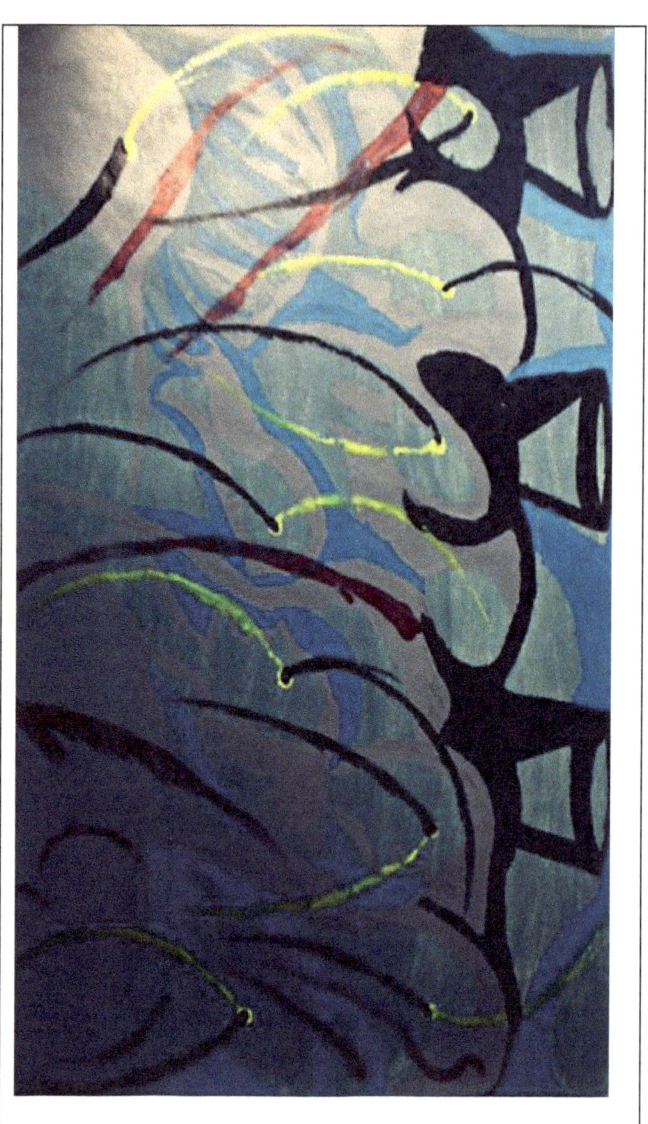

THAT LOVE

I have always known it is love
  Because it reveals itself openly
    For concealment betrays doubts.
      That love works with me
        In its many unusual ways.

Opening up along some love-line.
  Opening glimpses of attractive feelings
    And undiscovered emotions.
      Opening and opening and opening
        And I have the guts to follow that love.

That love envelops me in dry warmth.
  It is a place where I am so alive.
    That place can have a magic
      Whilst I am living it.
        And I know I would never love like that
          That it would never happen again.

That love is an infinitesimal tripod-
  Composed of flesh, feelings, and thoughts.
    That love is a singular multiplicity
      A thing of ultimate beauty
        That draws my deepest attentions.

That love which I feel-

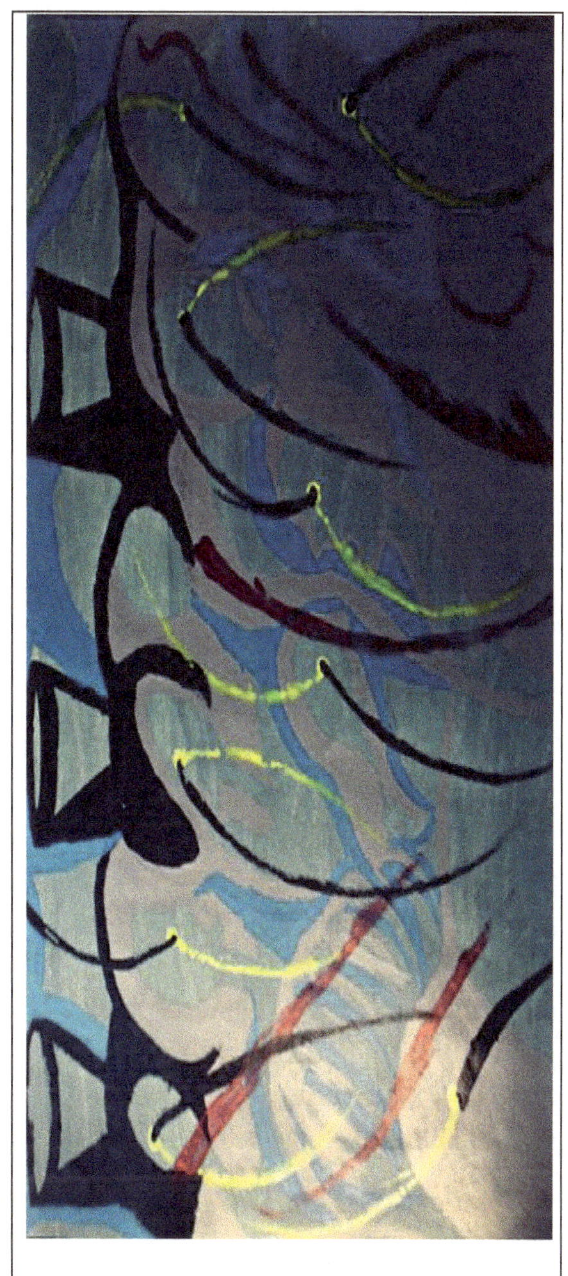

That love is a passionate intuition.
I see that love in my dreams.
My energies feasts upon that love
And she gets born, in my dreams.
She is in every realm
In any realm.

And I am the background that defines her
Like actions of polarities on each other.
She stands out against me
Like a full spectrum.
She is the evidence of my love for her.

And I have often watched her
Wrestling with things she can only feel
But cannot yet express.
And I could not stir
Lest I disturb her.
The physical shock of it all
Like a demanding thing.

She feels a compelling compassion
A thing that comes with our cells.
It is a current of human love
A need to share, to give whatever!

And she will provide the answers
As we go along.
She will fruit in the warmth of emotions

In the willingness to spent herself on-

That love which makes life sweet for giving.
That love which makes life warm.
That love which fills life with beauty.
That love I would cherish it for her.

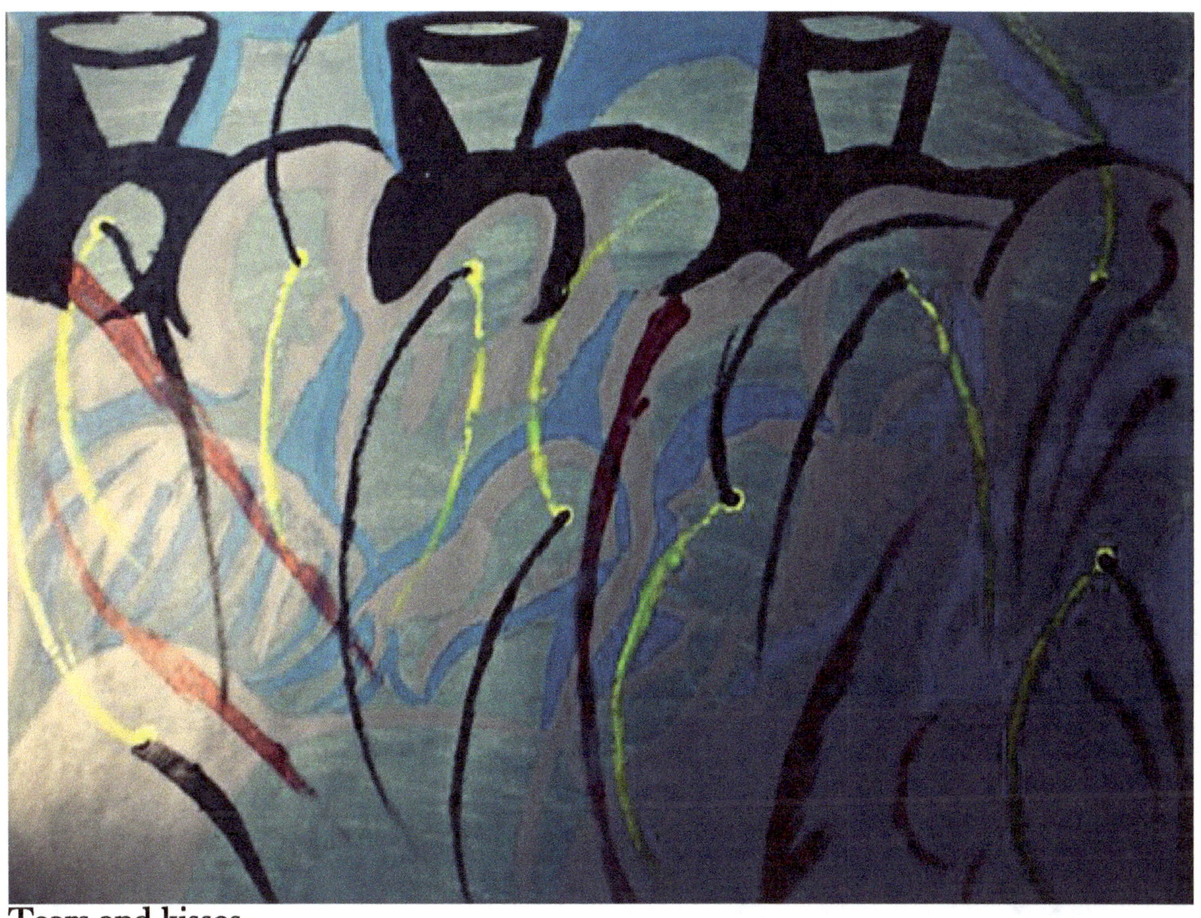

Tears and kisses

MEMORIES LIKE STONES

I count the words in the rain.
Raindrops in which,
A lifetime trembles to take shape.
And we walked that ever-shifting line-
Between the ocean and the land.
Measuring our own fragility-
Against the ways of the tides.

We remain dedicated to this pattern-
That reveals as much as it cancels.
Like nudity that hides inside itself.
Within which a life happened.
Which filled our senses-
Lingering on this beginning.

The days slipped away touched-
By the sun that sinks like a,
Song running through our hearts.
We were a song, yet-
We were trees most of our lives,
Of our necessary self-doms.
Perfection in things always missing.
Out of which we made sacrifices.
On raged-ends of human doubts.

Guide my hand to touch your heart,

Between the scars.
Leaping into tongues!

We entered into each other's menu.
Savouring sweetness for a living.
The soft shadows of your voice.
The voice you never learned to use.
The unspoken things within words.
We delved into experience and,
Reached for lives furrowed by sorrows.

Memories like stones, like-
Perennials coming back in summer.
Laughter opposes a sad breeze.
Like the way light enters a time.
Lighting our world on fire.

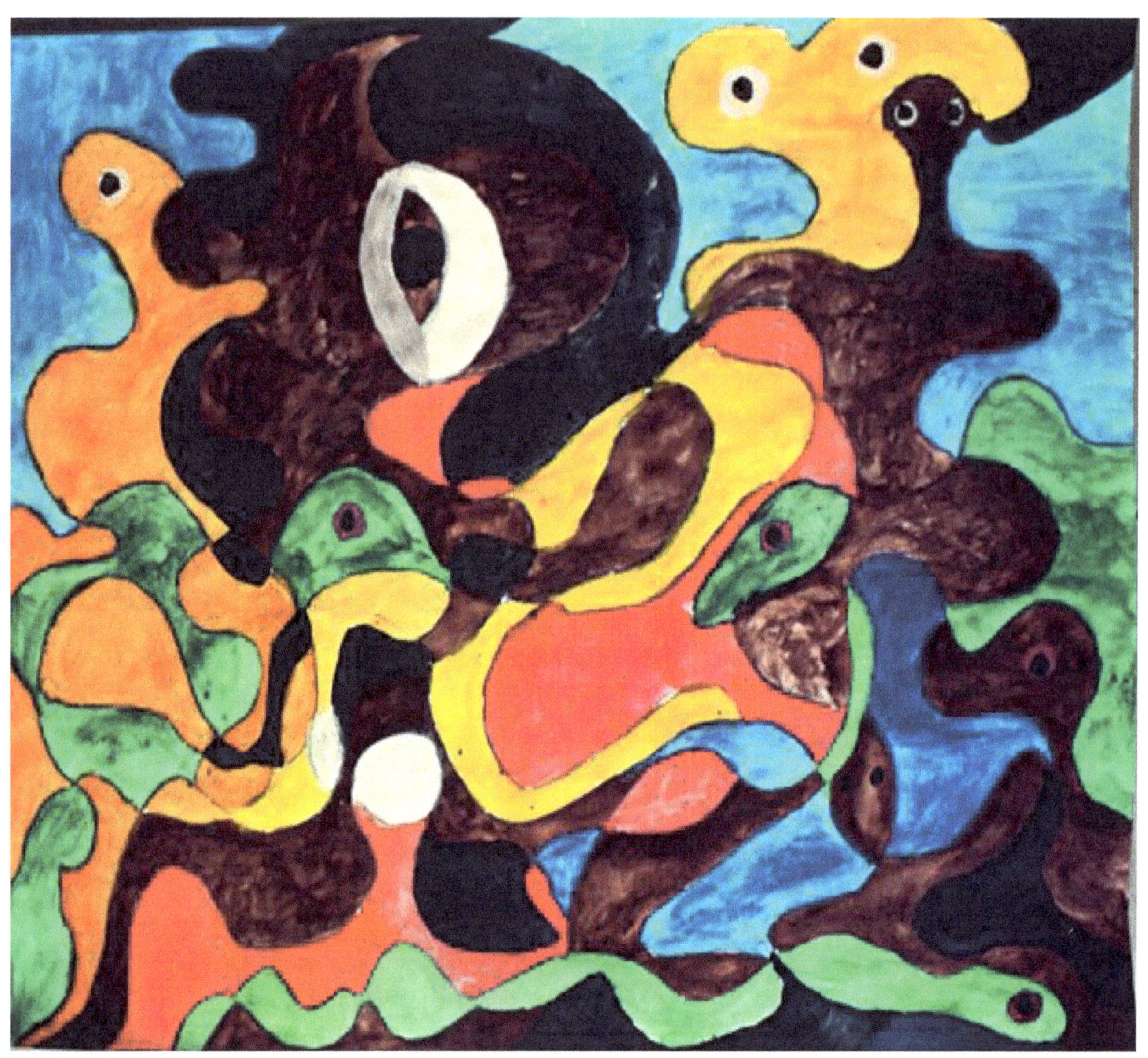

Animals prospectus

the eye of a bull

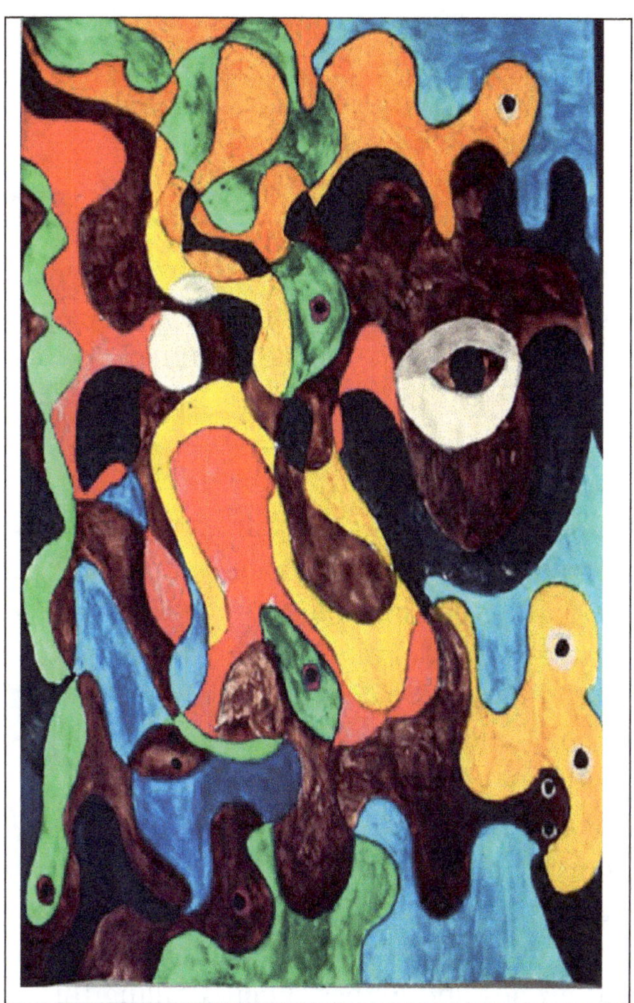

This week of waiting has been a bothersome one. It has been tarnished by cumuli-nimbus clouds of your mind's cloudy skies. You seemed like you were sited amidst the spinning sky; the quivering sun. This week you have also dissected the eye of the bull. You have also discovered that the bull was not pregnant. Demons also study the silent spaces of our lives. She phoned you last week: telling you that she is done with you. You remember you had said to her that you had heard that before. That you had used that several times when you were the uninterested one. The (unconvinced) one. You had also told her that she had become a network against your feelings. You had also asked to see her. She had said she would see you in a week's time. You hadn't been bothered by that mountain throughout that week. That network against your feelings; for you thought you had already sorted it. To be stubborn can encompass a mountain of stupidity too. But you couldn't help thinking; thinking the entire week about which soldiers were now on Patricia's side. Making love to her! And which were on your side. What uniforms were they wearing? It seemed all the soldiers were now wearing the same uniform. Patricia's uniform. Mocking you, laughing at you, gorging these new wound-sites of yours with their swords. With her words too!

patricia

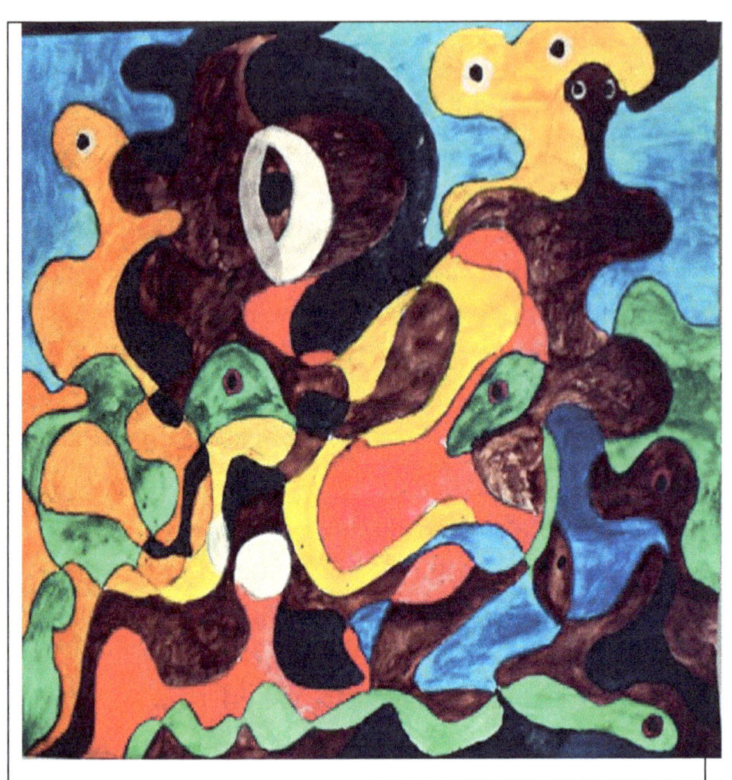

She tells you it's over again. Patricia says "no" to you and takes flight to the next yard. To the next human prospect. To the next sex prospect. To the next love prospect. You have discovered that it is too late. That she can take things away from you without a wink. Like the rain when it goes away. Taking things away with it; but also leaving some things behind. *What's wrong Patricia?* You ask her and she answers you using words. *Nothing José.* But you are all beyond the words you are using. There is only rhythm to the sound that is propelling you to use words. Your rainbow of happiness arches and arches and arches. Half is falling this way in the slathers of your anguish. Another half is falling that way to the hill. Falling behind the hill like a half frown. Like the colours of a childhood painful smile. These dances of lively rhythms are thoughts. Thoughts rich in un-speech; like the silent siren. You are so pink and raw. This rawness is stretching the tensions in the brittle chains of your thoughts. Happiness can be a dying mayfly!

grandmother

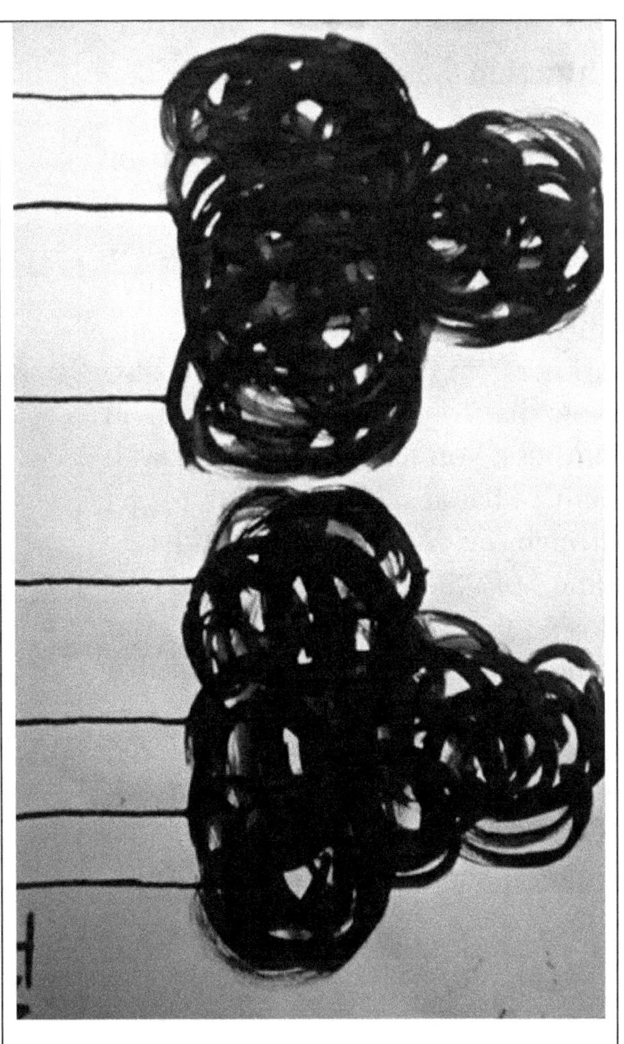

Your Grandmother says to you that love: Life and renewal leaves something else behind. An indelible mark. A memory of a time and place. A sweet taste. A time you were together with someone! She says that no matter how much erasure takes place; that there are always shadow impressions. Forms lurking and emerging in the dark. Grandmother also told you that loving someone is like the water throwing away its own soul; to be carried away only as liquid. A muddy liquid after a rainy day. Clogging everything. Only the muddy. Only the pain that you now feeling. She had said that we are guaranteed nothing. That we are assured of nothing other than hoping. And lying to ourselves that we always have all our love to give

Portraits in the darkness

You know you have been blown by this; into the next time zone. Like those things that comes up like portraits in the darkness. What man can measure and define the darkness in his heart? You also know that some of these portraits in darkness; you can learn to deal with them. That it's like for you to get through life you really have to let go some of these things. Especially those that hurt so bad. But grandmother had also told you; that if you have believed that what you have believed in was deeply rooted in the truth; that you didn't have to give up. Even if it meant standing alone. Or threatening your very existence!

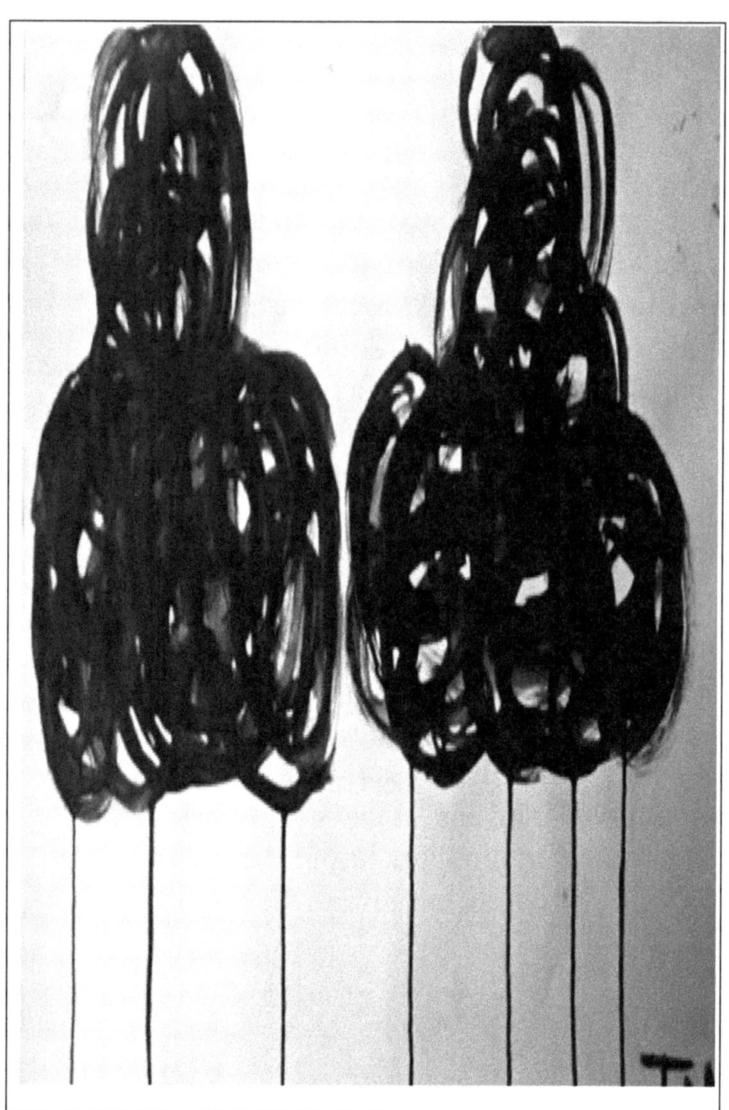

the language of the truth

But you let this story breathe itself out. You let the story write itself. In the language of the truth to your grandmother. But also in a language of double helixes of this truth to yourself. You tell your grandmother that your life is now like a house. A house unbuilding itself. A life in which you have raked what was dead from the ground. Displaced it! But lost a bigger part of yourself in the detritus? The cherry to garnish this cocktail was only one. Like the baptism in the Jordan; you know there is no half-way to it. But only full immersion. That you could only become the person your grandmother was talking of. But that it would be with a little curtsy. That you had to let her go.

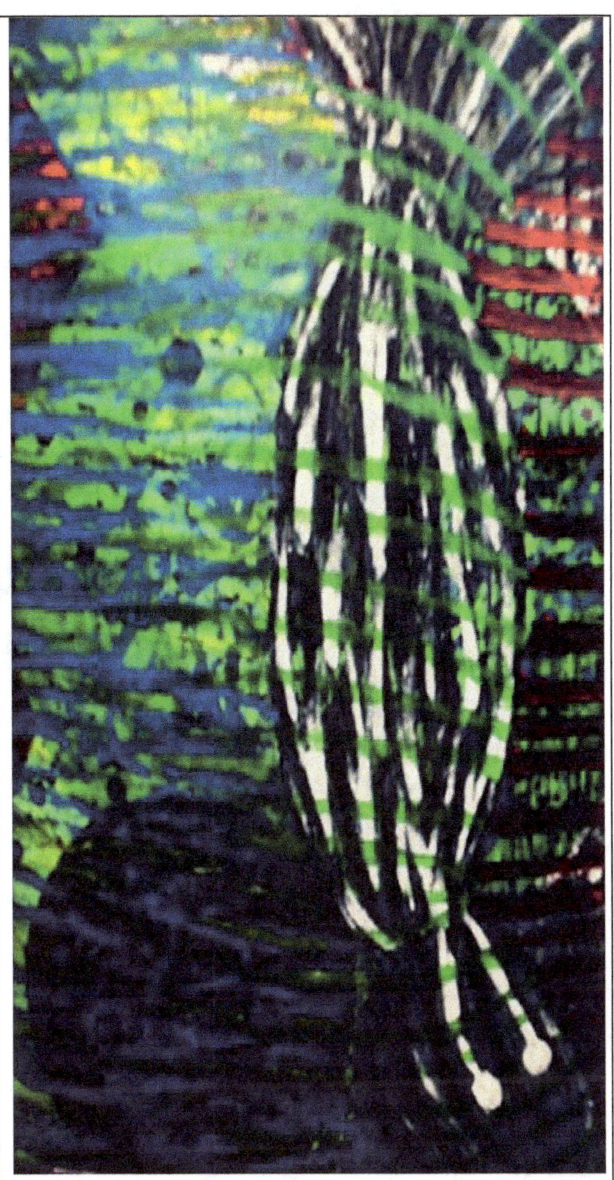

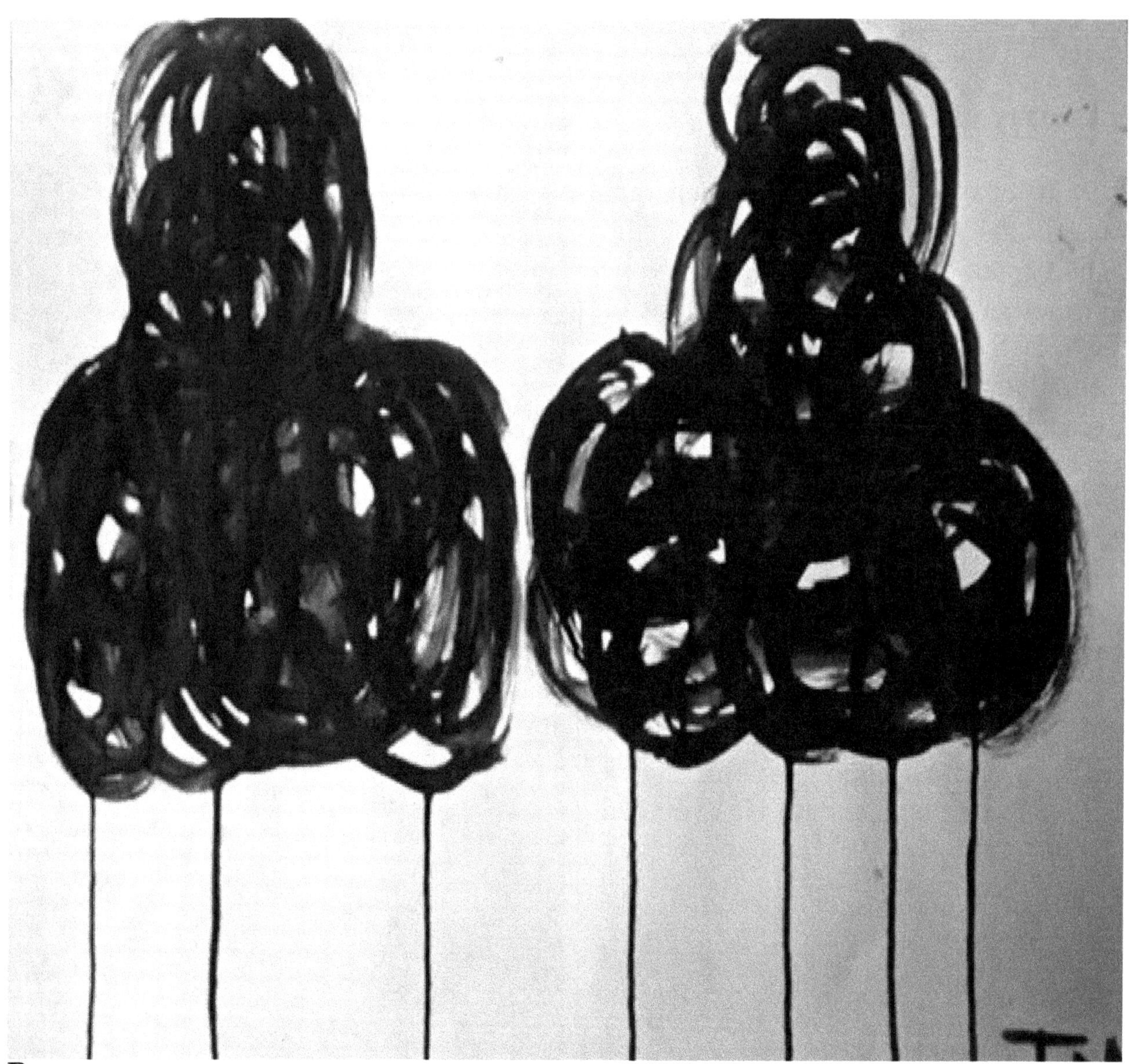

Partners

LOVE IS A LONELY CHOICE

Love is usually frozen in patterns
Love as a pattern of patterns
And I have used love to unlock
Patterns of another love
And I have set my pattern of it

We are always offered many choices
Only where its description is concerned
There are many words for love
A word for its intended use

For its chemical properties
Whether it comes honestly
Or from the black market
And for the belsen of its after-tastes

Whether it is dower's gift
Or from male or female
And for its age and colour
Your choices name your love

There is love of the soul
love of the flesh
There is love of the myth
And love of the reason
It is always a different thing

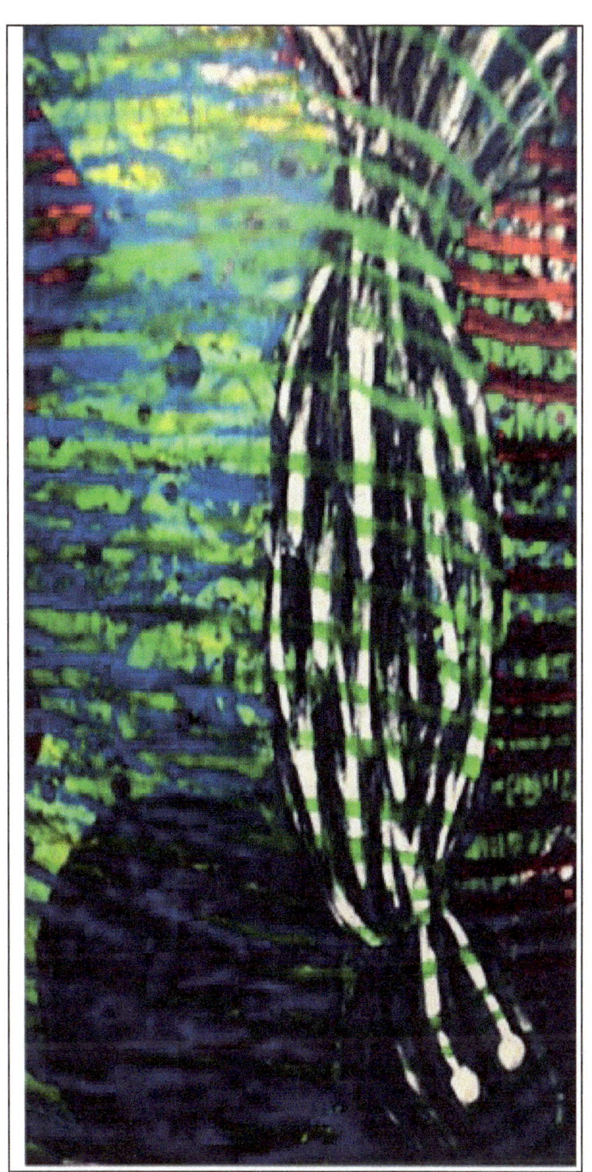

To each of us.

We want every sound
Every smell
The shapes and names
The colours
Even the tingling on our skins
And we also fear its other effects

Was Eve enough for Adam?
We are beginning to doubt everyone
But ourselves, of-course
No love is ever enough
The conditions don't permit it
It is always a matter of choice
A single, lonely choice.

When love is above its own laws
So many injuries occurs in love
Thus the need for some patterns
And prisons are often useful
We have a festive use of them
Love as punishment for sins

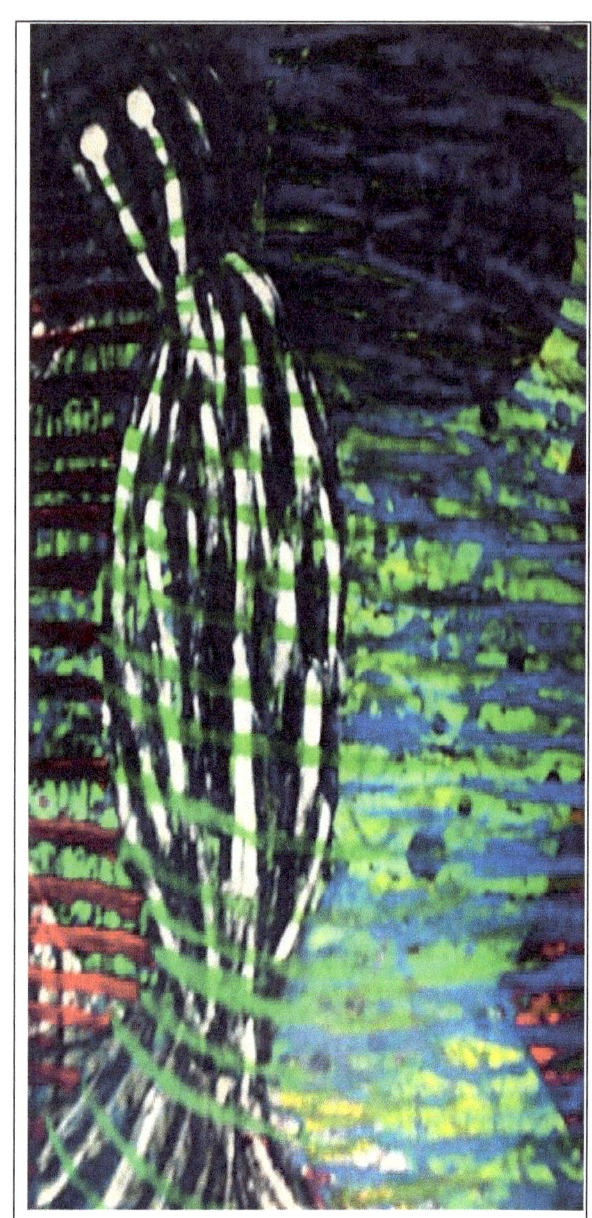

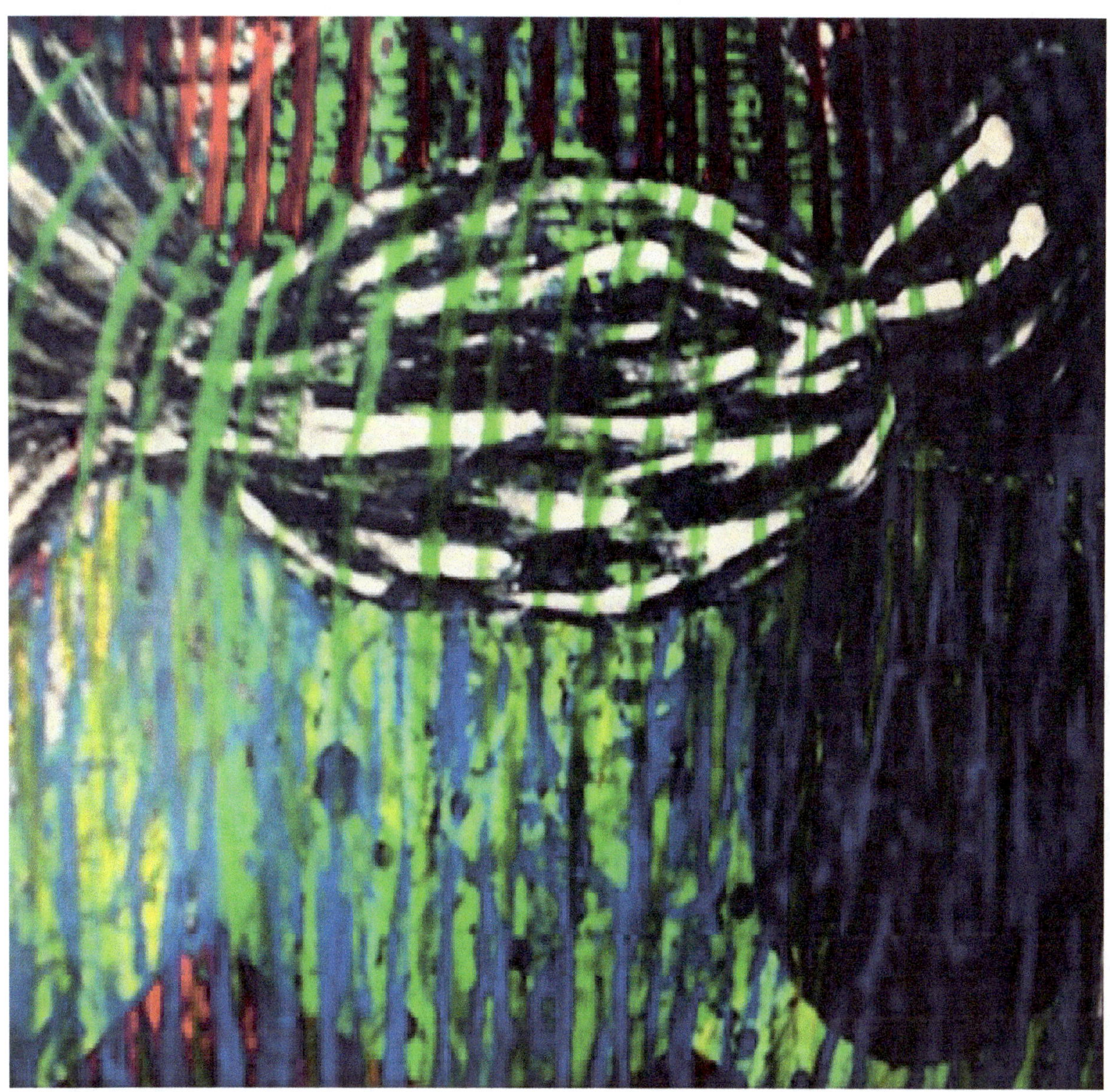

Bundle of love

FORCES

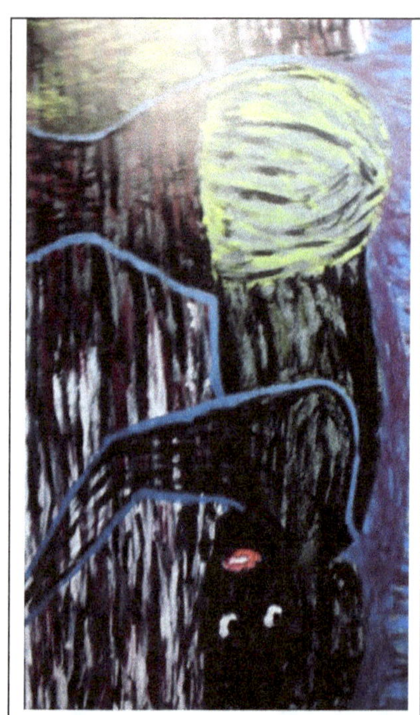

There are forces we understand in life.
There are forces we won't understand in life.
These forces come upon us every day in our life.
Most of these forces would never try to understand us.
They wouldn't even try to know us,
just a little bit, to begin us.

All that we could hope for is
that all that we have given
all that we really are
would someday suffice enough
to light the way for us.

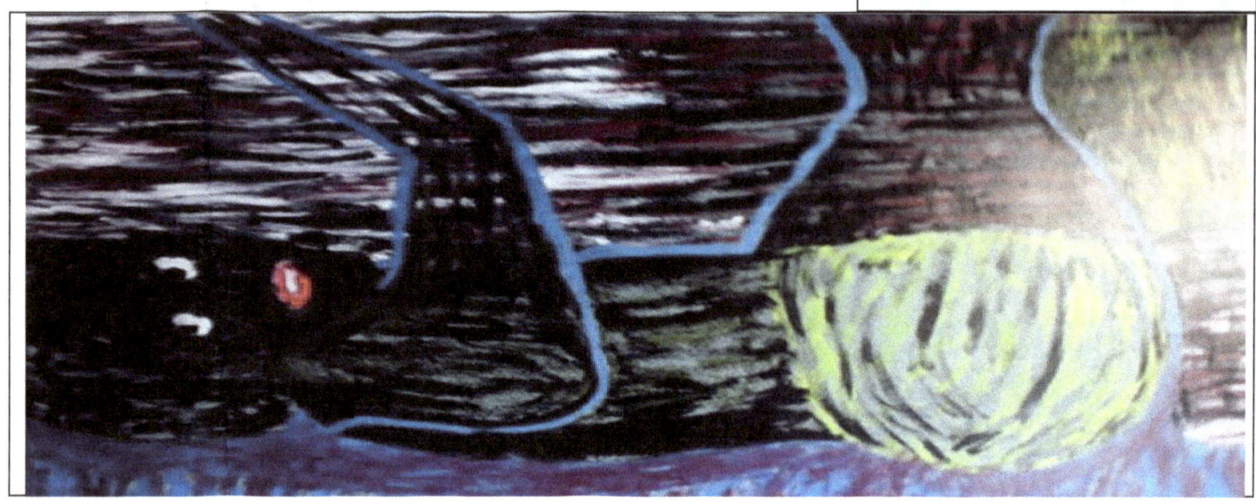

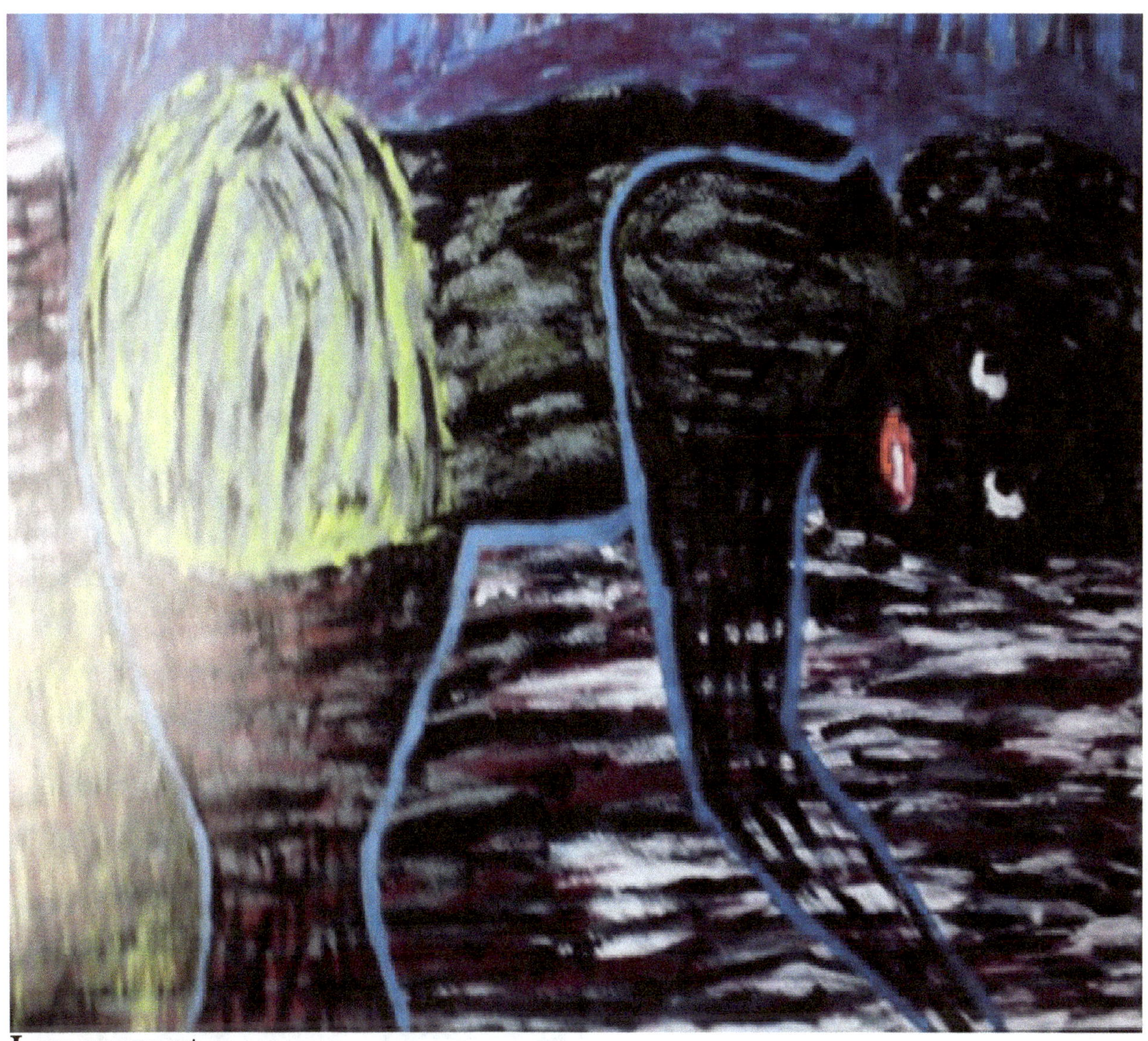

Love prospect

AT THAT MOMENT

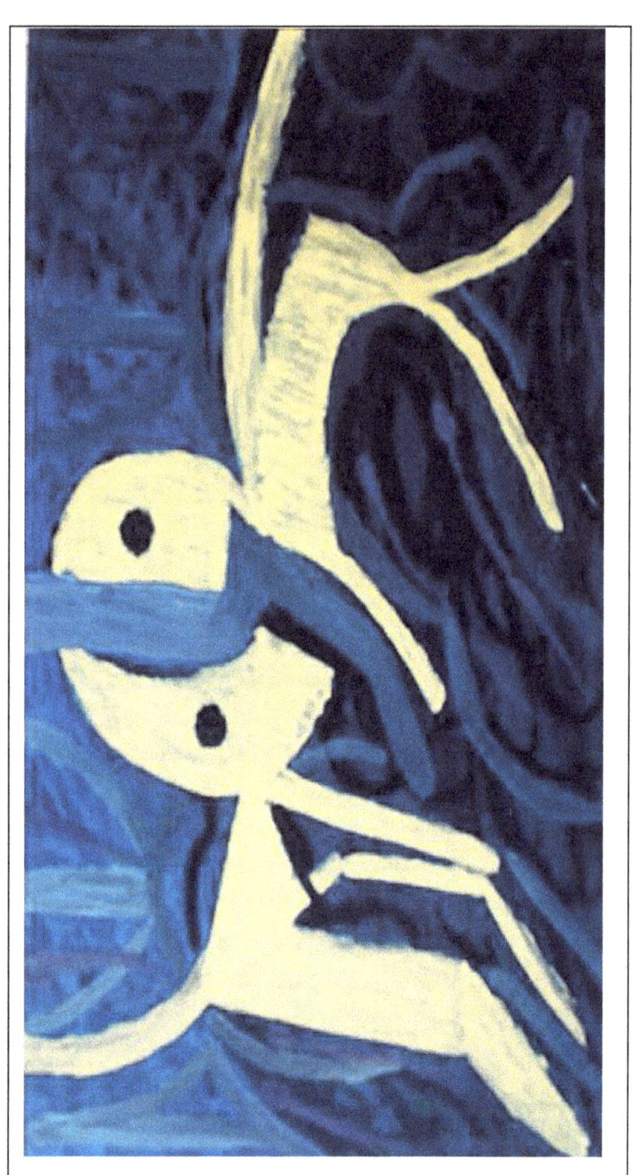

at that moment
it didn't play skirls
when coming for her
she didn't know
it was coming for her,
neither was it silent.

at that moment
every part of her body loomed
with attention and questions,
wide open.

at that moment
with no central line or point
but a deeper insertion
into her flesh, and its dangling
painful conduits were treading
on her inner road.

at that moment
it was this road
she has to pass through
in her all-consuming-mad-journey
out of this existence, within this existence
just a peripatetic existence, within this time.

HE CAN NOW SPEAK OF BEAUTY

Removing
the skins off this museum piece,
the peace he has developed
over the years

Pulling each of these flecks
like as if he is pulling the rose's
blossoms

in this very instance
it crosses his mind that
some people throw all their lives
into the river

that other people
will be throwing pebbles
into the same river,

that some people
will be throwing coins into the river
when others will be throwing keys.

soft keys,
are sounds of the water
hitting small obstructions in the river?

the watercolour shape

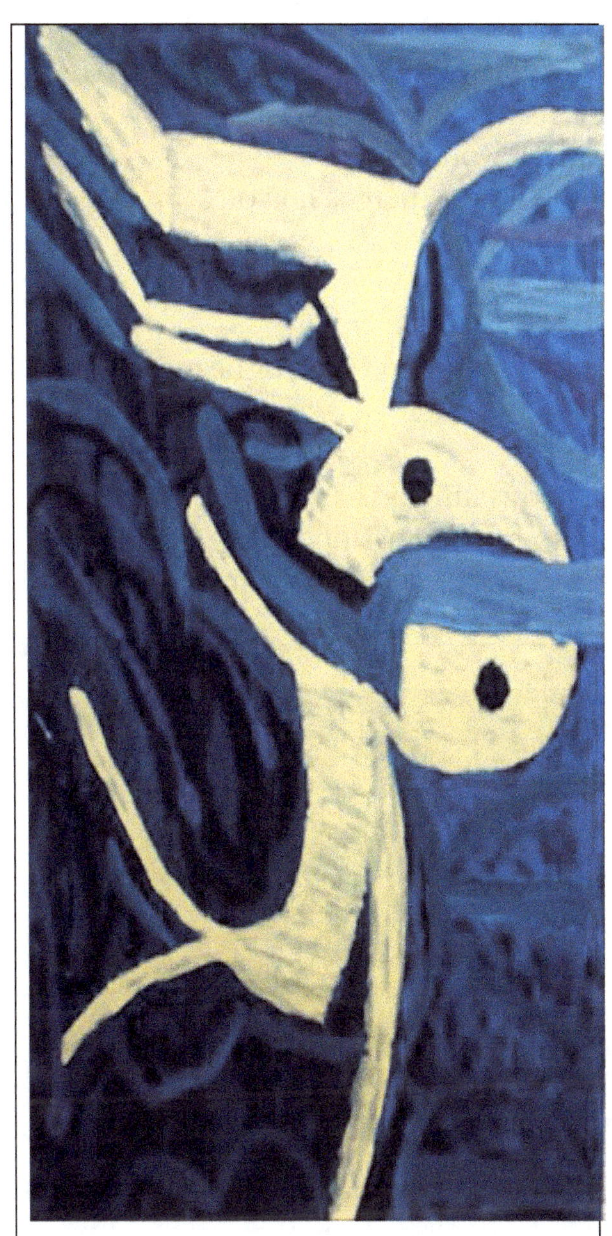

of their hearts
spreading in the river

without words
in the waters there is no voice
left behind for anyone
to listen to.

he knows he can speak of beauty
He knows the waters are now clear.

That this time he has decided
not to force things upon her
but to let her do the reaching out.

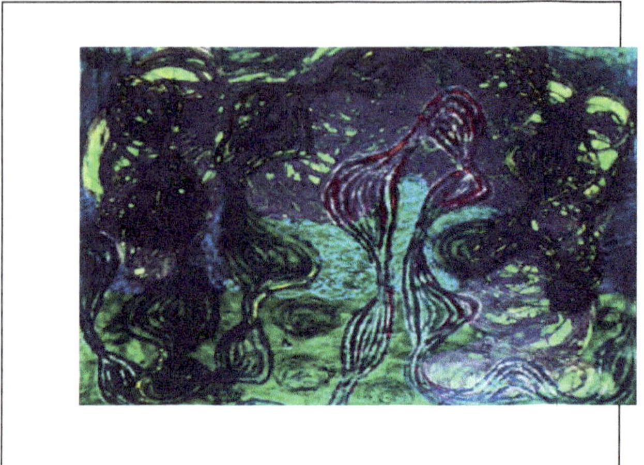

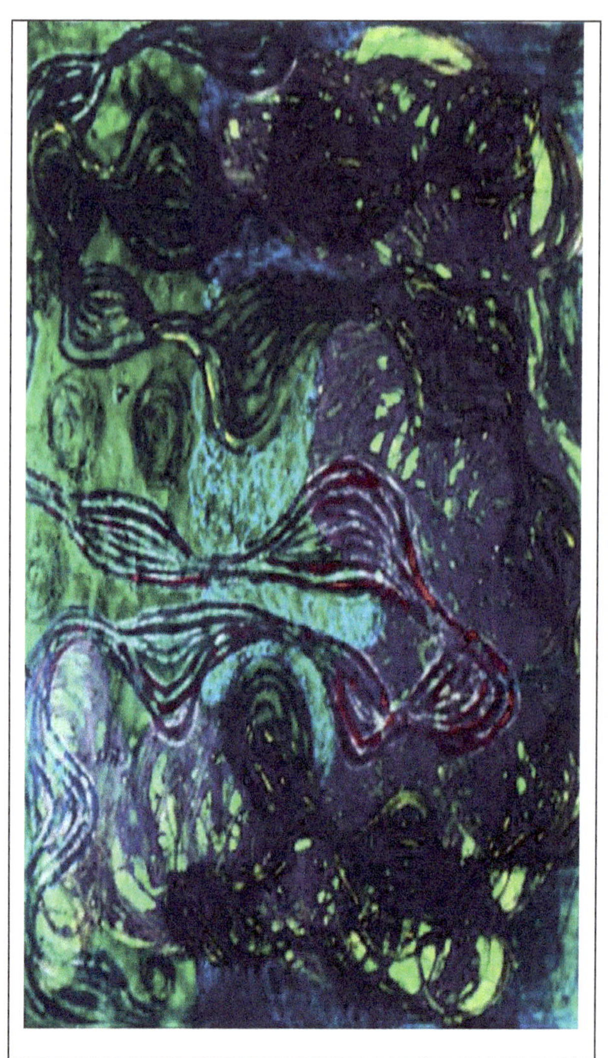

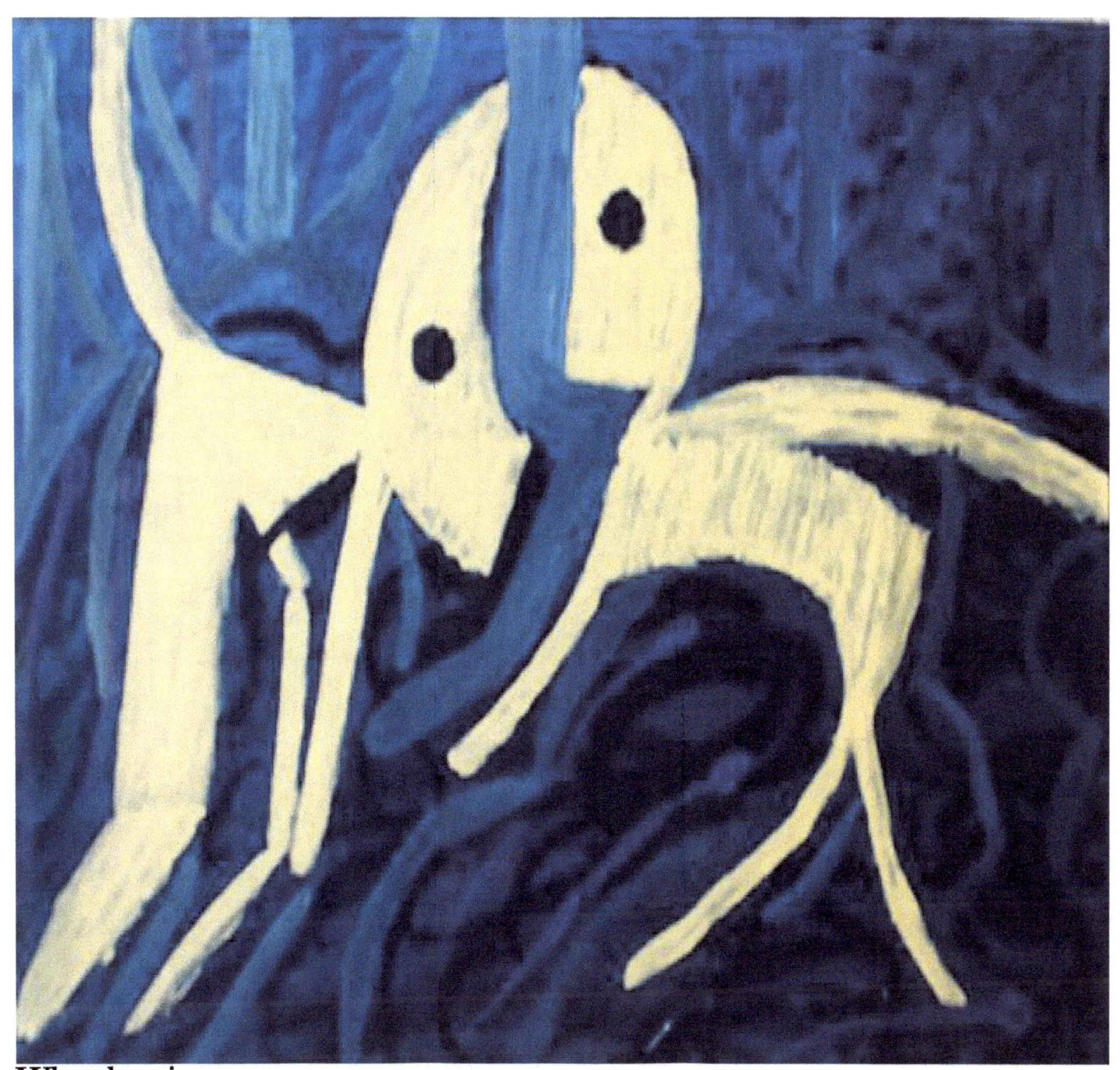
When love is gone

THEY START ON IT

he holds her
in his mouth,
a weight syrupy
on his tongue.

they start on it
and their hungers
deep in their stomachs

are manual
lawnmowers,
laborious
primitive
bequeathing
bequeathing...

Are
manual
lawnmowers,
laborious
primitive
bequeathing
bequeathing
bequeathing
bequeathing

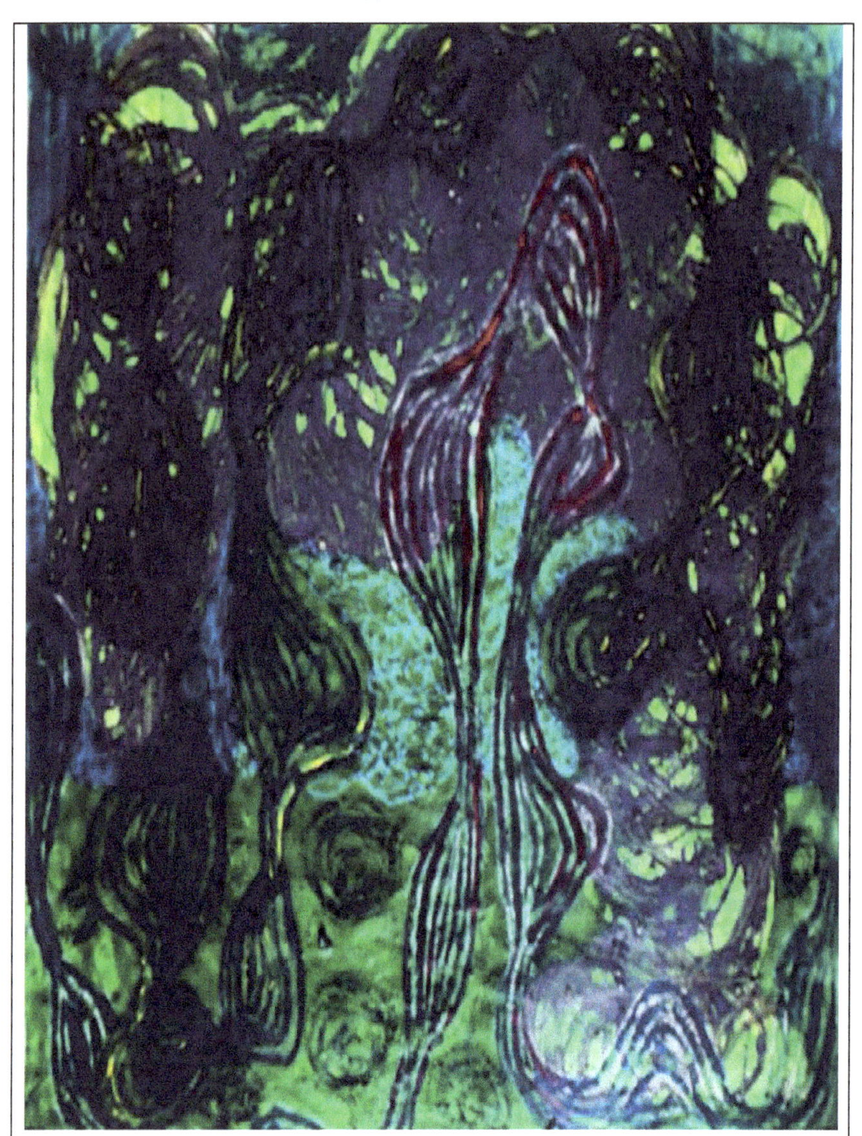

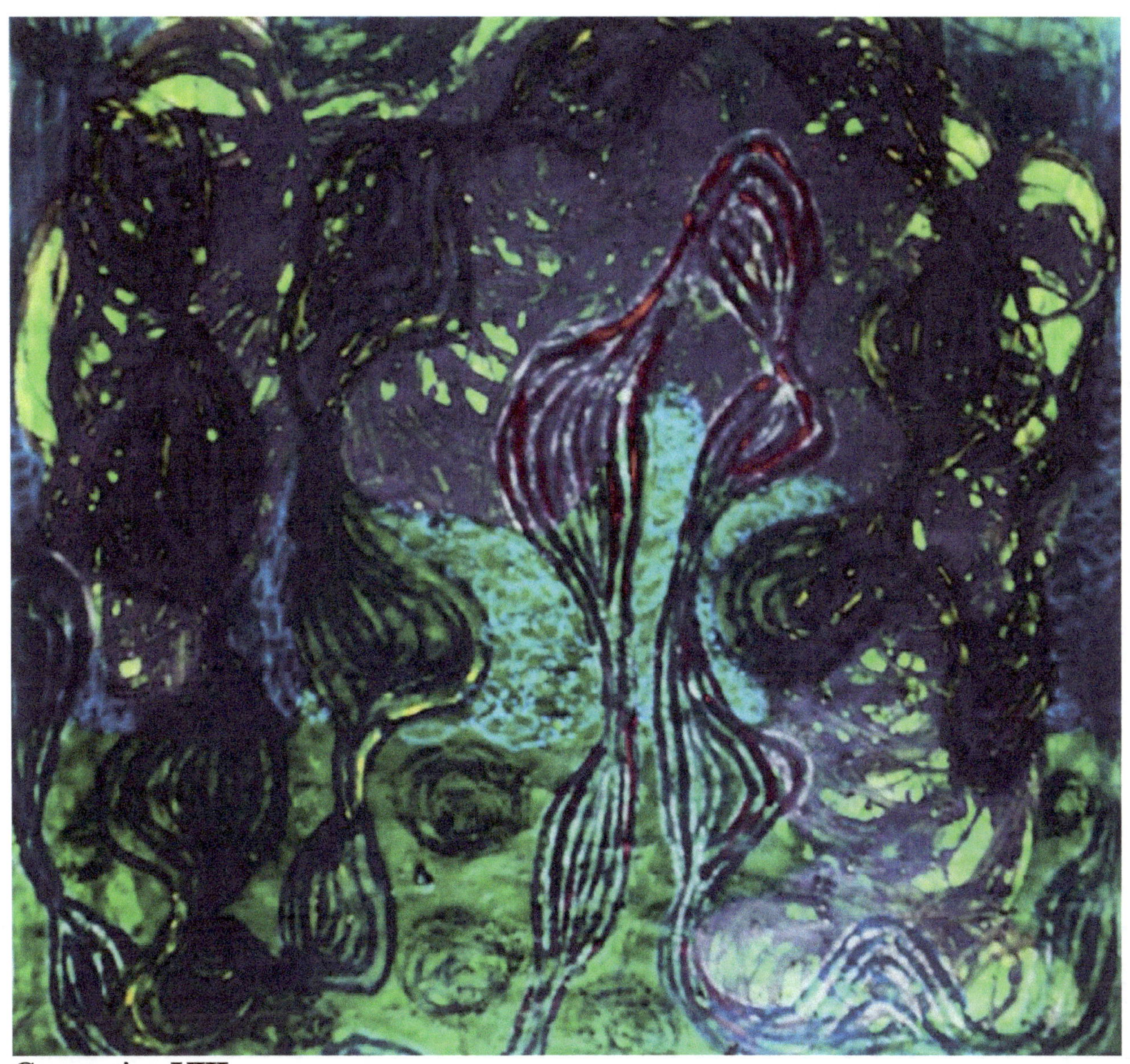

Connection VIII

SHADOWS

The sun
up the skies
is a dragon's
eyes

spreading
its scaly tails,
moving.

the shadows
on her face

broken sun's
light
floating.

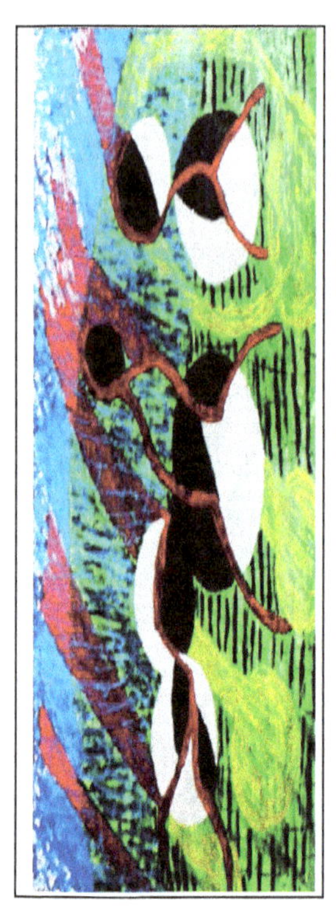

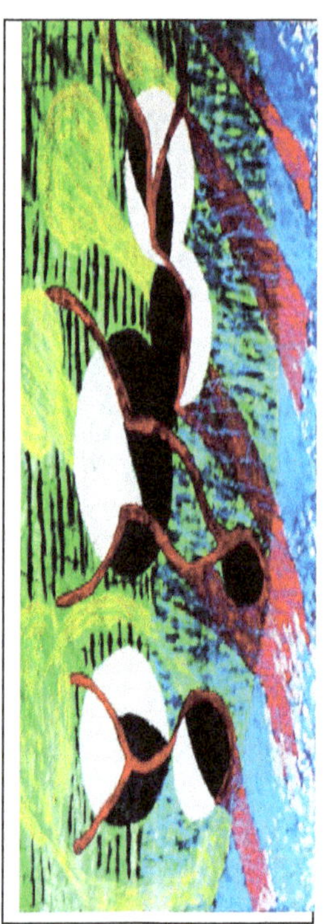

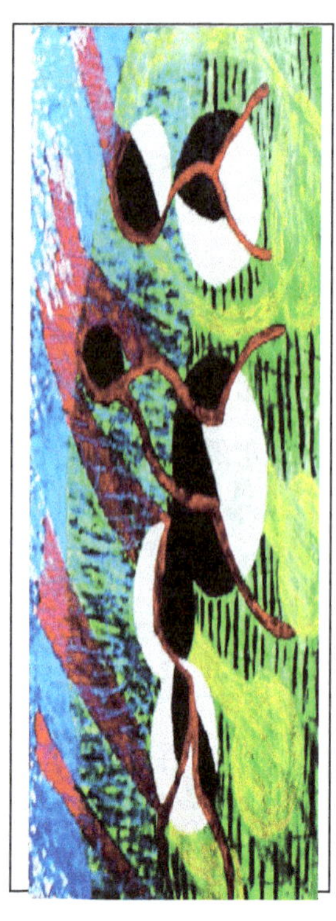

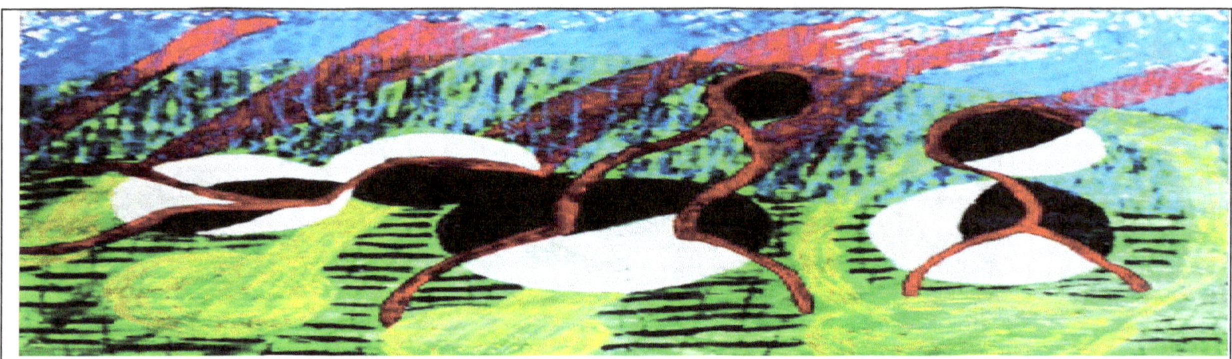

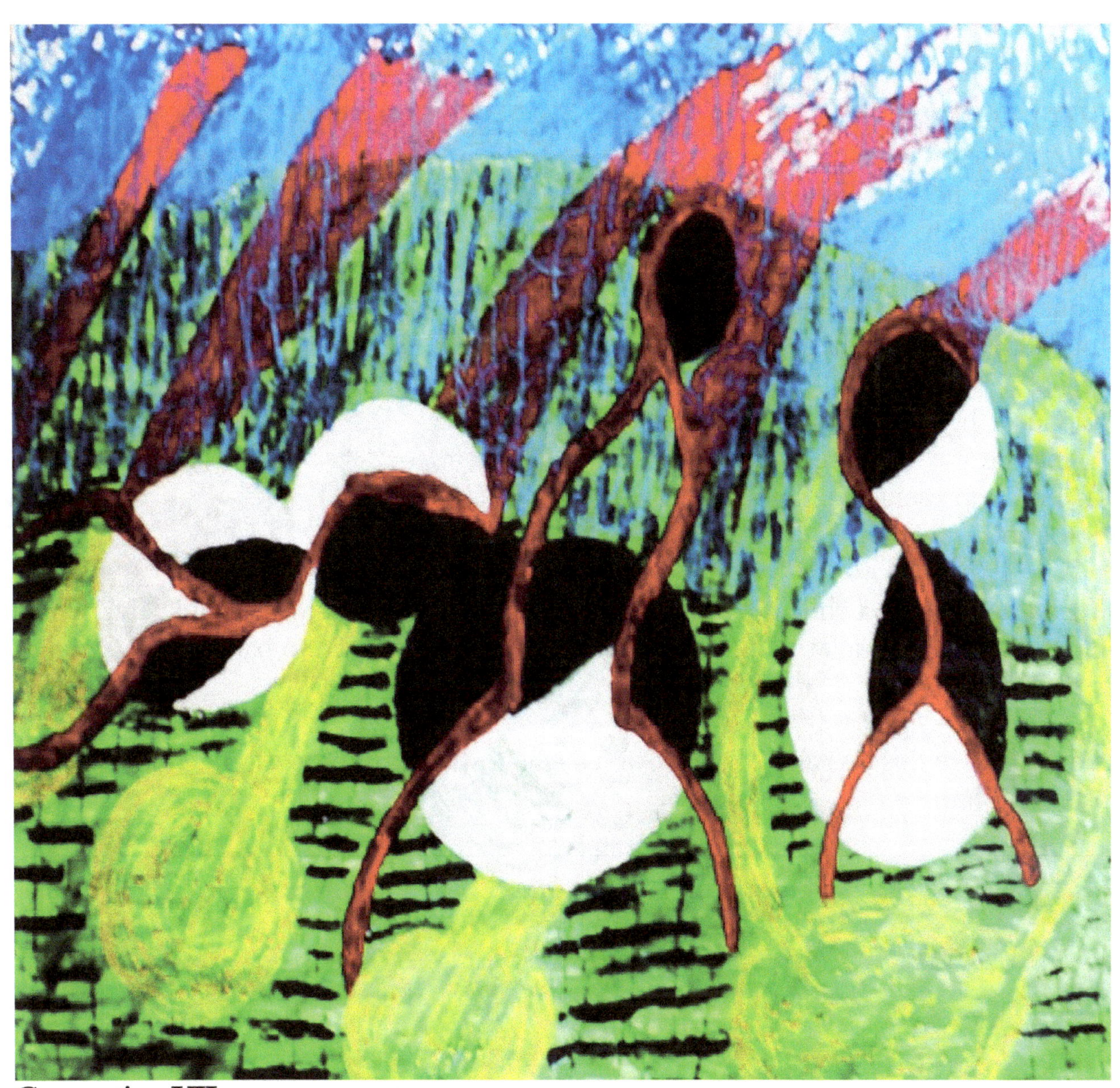

Connection VII

UPTO NOW

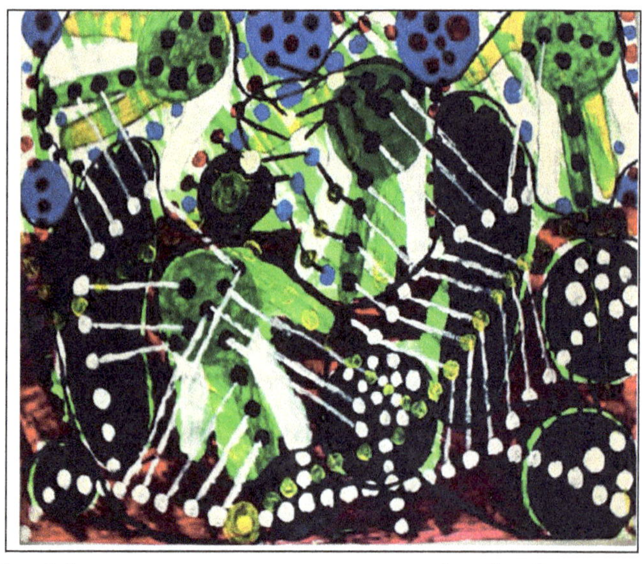

Upto now he knows you still haven't figured out why he avoided you after the prayers that day, why he left you with your Auntie, why he left for home, alone even though it was raining that evening.

Upto now he knows you haven't figured out that he was so scared of you, of what you now represented to him, of how he felt for you.

He had never been a child, all his life and, for him to now trust you completely the way he did was to part away with bits of himself that he never wanted to part with, in order to make room for you.

The balance of this loss and whatever of his reach, still left in him, was like the colour of absence to him.

He had never been a child, all his life and, for him to now trust you completely the way he did was to part away with bits of himself that he never wanted to part with, in order to make room for you.

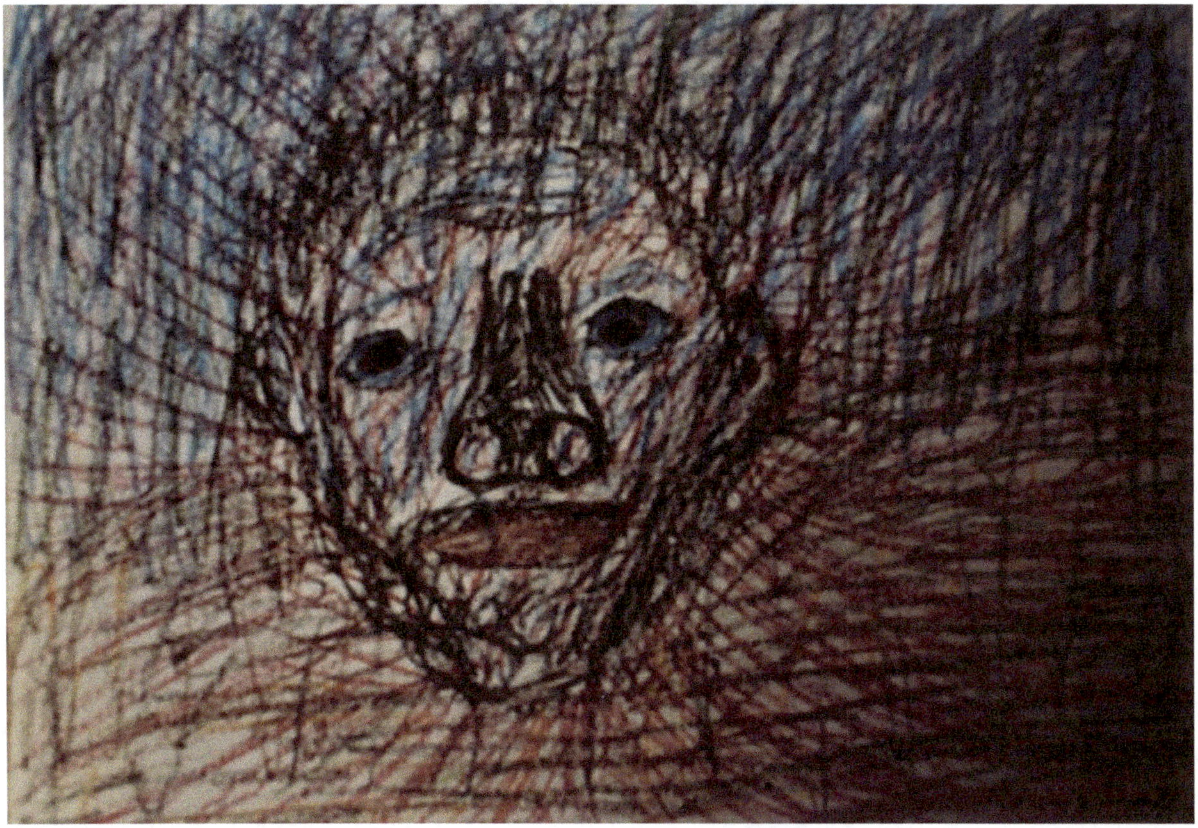

He burns

UNNAMEABLE WOUND

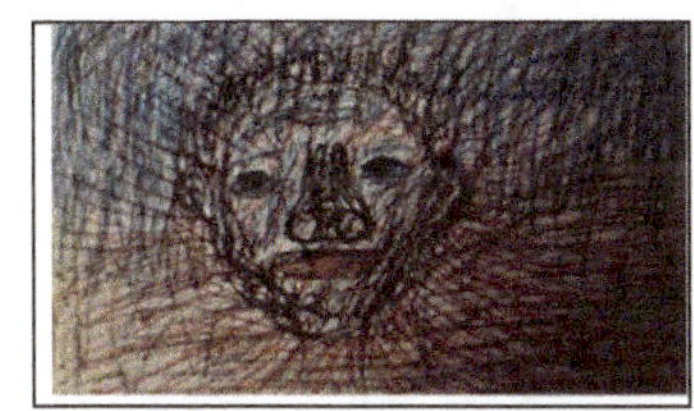

he had the anti-Jesus
the Sadducees' heart
the Pharisees' head
in his heart, the bullets

in his head, they pelted
her with painful
flames of disbelief
non-commitment,
un-satisfaction.

the pop of those bullets
on her heart,
on her frame
burned holes
dusty holes
of ash
of smoke
of fire

too much pain
too much suffering
never felt before.
a pain like that took
awhile to heal.

a pain like that is
some unnameable
wound that scars the soul...

a pain like that
she could only learn,
to grow and adapt
but it never goes away

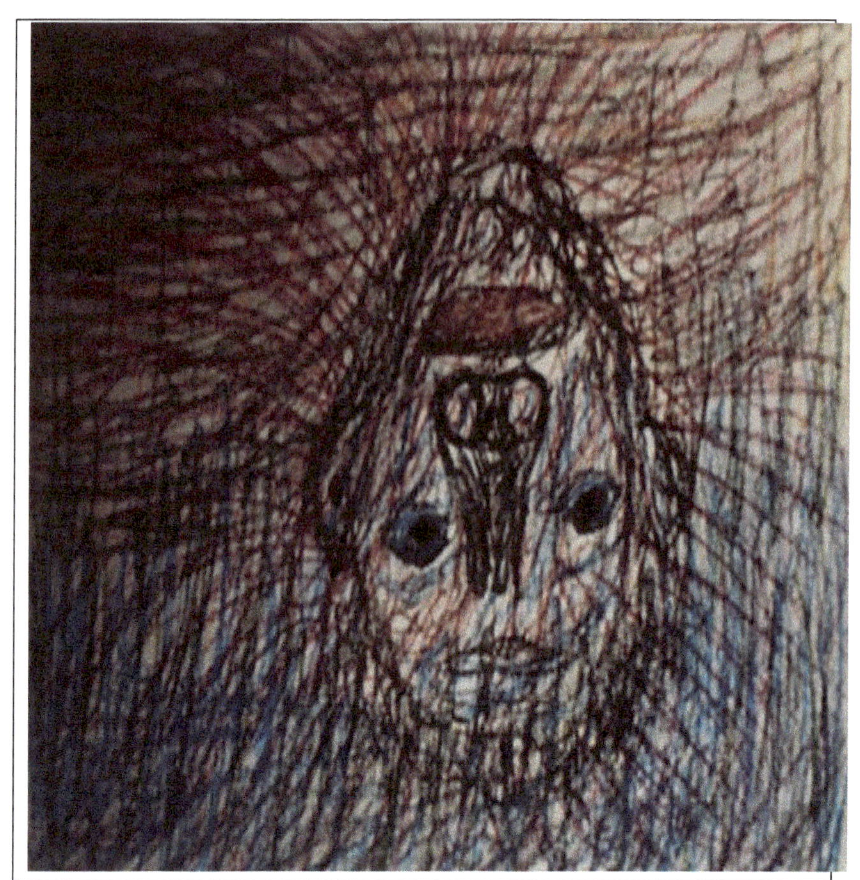

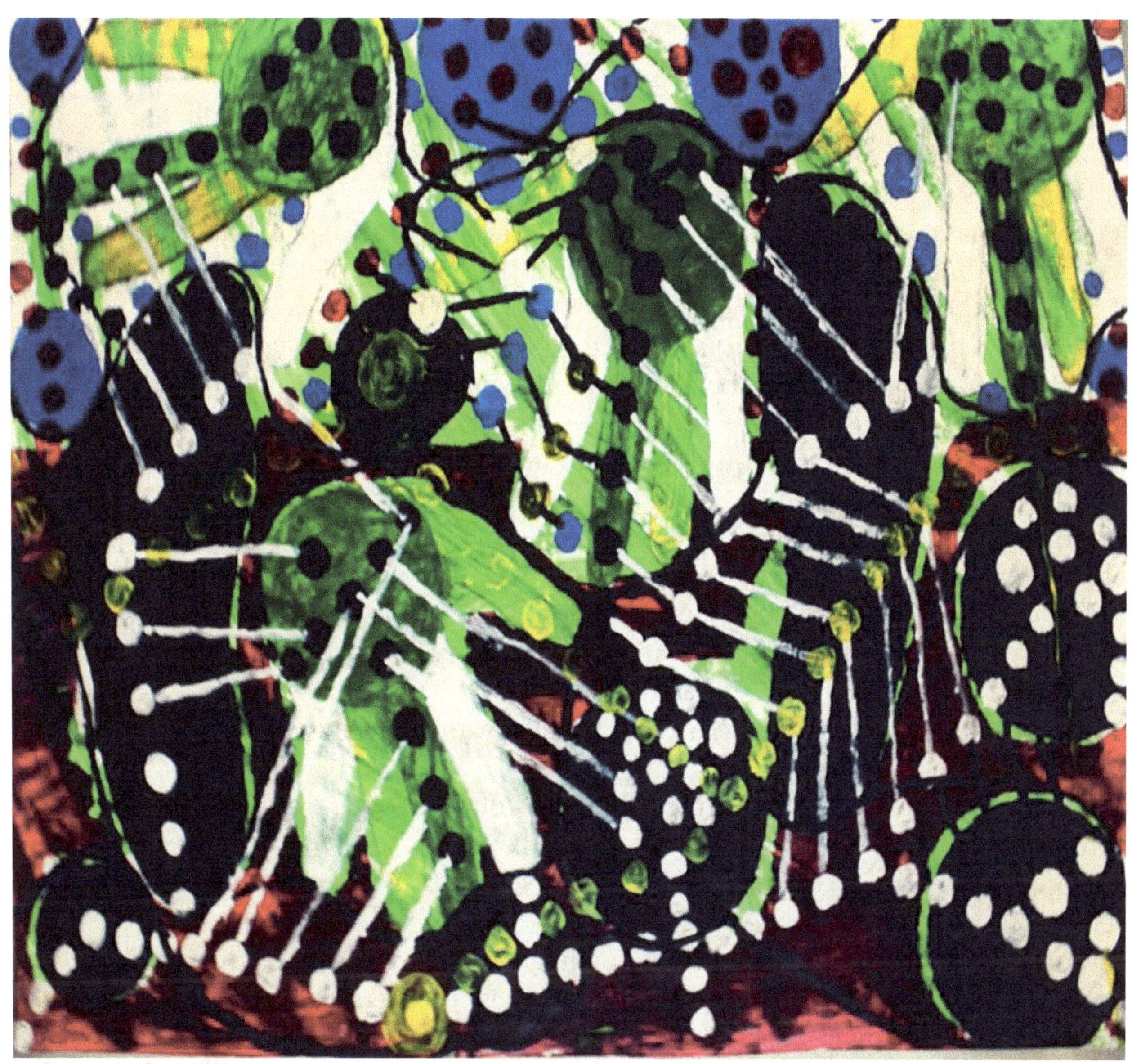

Connection VI

Love means

When love has come to mean you are not a fool
When love has come to mean they don't make you feel jealous of yourself
When love has come to mean you are not hunters walking in the empty fields looking for yourselves
When love has come to mean chasing the butterflies till your shadows are out of breath
When love has come to mean you mobilise the bees to dance in the wind whilst creating honey for your love
When love has come to mean you recruit the birds to sing love songs for your love
When love has come to mean being a child drawing figures we want to make alive and hold in the sandy roads
When love has come to mean the roads to our hearts we have opened for our love to walk back to us
When love has come to mean seeing the flight of bird's feathers dancing in the wind with joy for you, as the nurse of your luck
When love has come to mean living with them like a heartbeat
When love has come to mean knowing all the notes of your heart's crescendos to the sight of her
When love has come to mean your chest swelling with concertos of the after bridge of a love song
When love has come to mean seeing golden rays of joy flowing over her face like tender mercies
When love has come to mean you wake every morning to roses that make thorns look green in the eyes of your love
When love has come to mean walking holding hands in the ghetto streets without fuss like that olden Manyame park couple I see every morning; walking silently, holding hands, wallowing in their internal heaven, their faces orgasmic wonder!
When love has come to mean soaring in air to sublimity and the impossible

When love has come to mean a river that gently argues against barriers flowing through you like that olden couple of Nyatate who can't stop arguing, messing around each other like pfurikanyi (sibling rivalry), and yet still can't do without each other

When love has come to mean the emotional vastness that touches the mountains with humility

When love has come to mean as the years percolates your drying wrinkled soils you grow younger inside to fight the fear of the dying frame.

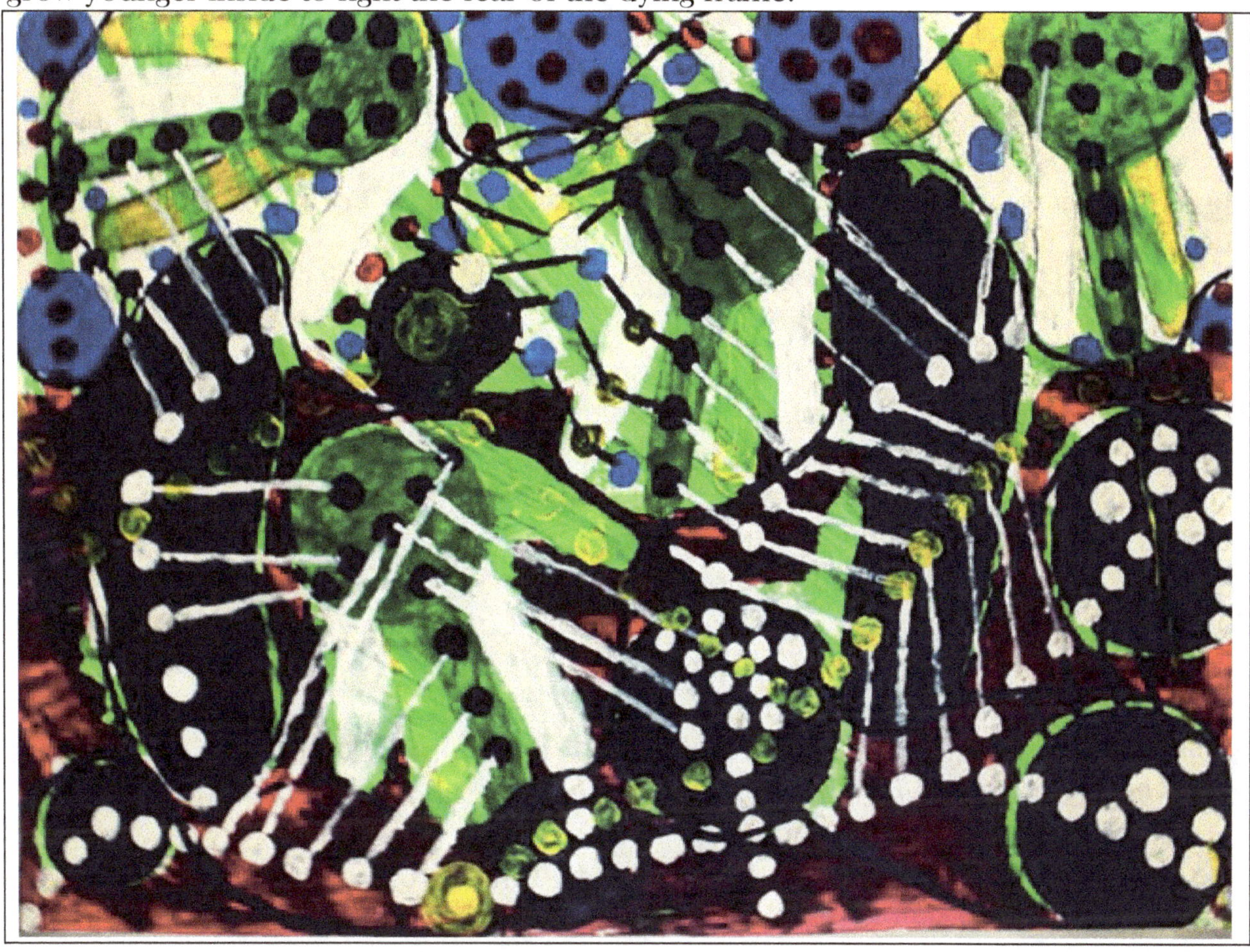

Mmap Multi-disciplinary Series

If you have enjoyed *Glyphs of Love,* consider these other fine books in the **Mmap Multi-disciplinary Series** from *Mwanaka Media and Publishing:*

Africanization and Americanization Anthology Volume 1, Searching for Interracial, Interstitial, Intersectional and Interstates Meeting Spaces, Africa Vs North America by Tendai R Mwanaka
A Conversation..., A Contact by Tendai Rinos Mwanaka
Africa, UK and Ireland: Writing Politics and Knowledge Production Vol 1 by Tendai R Mwanaka
Writing Language, Culture and Development, Africa Vs Asia Vol 1 by Tendai R Mwanaka, Wanjohi wa Makokha and Upal Deb
Zimbolicious: An Anthology of Zimbabwean Literature and Arts, Vol 3 by Tendai Mwanaka
Drawing Without Licence by Tendai R Mwanaka
Writing Grandmothers/ Escribiendo sobre nuestras raíces: Africa Vs Latin America Vol 2 by Tendai R Mwanaka and Felix Rodriguez
Tiny Human Protection Agency by Megan Landman
Ghetto Symphony by Mandla Mavolwane
A Portrait of Defiance by Tendai Rinos Mwanaka
Nationalism: (Mis)Understanding Donald Trump's Capitalism, Racism, Global Politics, International Trade and Media Wars, Africa Vs North America Vol 2 by Tendai R Mwanaka
Ouafa and Thawra: About a Lover From Tunisia by Arturo Desimone
Zimbolicious: An Anthology of Zimbabwean Literature and Arts, Vol 4 by Tendai Mwanaka and Jabulani Mzinyathi
Chitungwiza Mushamukuru Anthology by Tendai Rinos Mwanaka
The Day and the Dweller: A Study of the Emerald Tablets by Jonathan Thompson

Zimbolicious: An Anthology of Zimbabwean Literature and Arts, Vol 5 by Tendai Mwanaka
Robotics Anthology, Africa vs Asia Vol 2 by Tendai Rinos Mwanaka
Shaping Up by Tendai Rinos Mwanaka
Zimbolicious Anthology Vol 6: An Anthology of Zimbabwean Literature and Arts by Tendai Rinos Mwanaka and Chenjerai Mhondera
Registers of Loss: PhotoTalking to the Baobab Trees of Nyatate by Tendai Rinos Mwanaka
The Trick is to Keep Breathing: Covid 19 Stories From African and North American Writers, vol 3 by Tendai Rinos Mwanaka
Fixing Earth: An Anthology of Ireland, UK and Africa Writers, Vol 2 by Tendai Rinos Mwanaka
Zimbolicious: An Anthology of Zimbabwean Literature and Arts, Vol 7 Tendai Rinos Mwanaka and Tanaka Chidora
Writing Woman Anthology: Personal Essays and Short stories, An Anthology of African and Asian Writers, Vol 3 by Tendai Rinos Mwanaka, Abigail George, Sue Zhu and Monalisa Jena
Writing Woman Anthology: Drama and Scholarly Essays, An Anthology of African and Asian Writers, Vol 3 by Tendai Rinos Mwanaka, Abigail George, Sue Zhu and Monalisa Jena
WRITING WOMAN ANTHOLOGY: Poetry and Visual art by Tendai Rinos Mwanaka, Abigail George, Sue Zhu and Monalisa Jena
Zimbolicious: An Anthology of Zimbabwean Literature and Arts, Vol 8 by Tendai Rinos Mwanaka and Matthew Kunashe Chikono
Of poets, gods, ghosts. Irritants and storytellers by Tendai Rinos Mwanaka
The Aporia of Unnamed Things by Tendai Rinos Mwanaka

Upcoming

Men: An Anthology of African and Latin American writers vol 3 by Tendai Rinos Mwanaka and Ingrid Bringas

https://facebook.com/MwanakaMediaAndPublishing/

www.ingramcontent.com/pod-product-compliance
Lightning Source LLC
LaVergne TN
LVHW081252100826
845148LV00009B/1205

* 9 7 8 1 7 7 9 3 3 8 6 1 7 *